NICHOLSON

G000166451

LONDON

KEY TO MAP PAGES

PRIMROSE HILL

CAMDEN TOWN · KING'S CROSS · ISLINGTON · HOXTON

REGENT'S PARK · PENTONVILLE

ST. PANCRAS · FINSBURY · SHOREDITCH

MARYLEBONE · EUSTON ROAD · BLOOMSBURY · CLERKENWELL

PADDINGTON · LONDON WALL

WESTBOURNE GREEN · OXFORD STREET · SOHO · HOLBORN · CITY

BAYSWATER · STRAND

BAYSWATER ROAD · MAYFAIR · ALDWYCH · VICTORIA EMBANKMENT

KENSINGTON · HYDE PARK · KENSINGTON GARDENS · PICCADILLY · ST. JAMES'S · SOUTHWARK

HOLLAND PARK · KENSINGTON HIGH STREET · KNIGHTSBRIDGE · GREEN PARK · ST. JAMES'S PARK · WATERLOO · BOROUGH · OLD KENT ROAD

SOUTH KENSINGTON · WESTMINSTER · NEWINGTON · BERMONDSEY

CROMWELL ROAD · KNIGHTSBRIDGE · BELGRAVIA · BELGRAVE RD · LAMBETH

BROMPTON ROAD · PIMLICO

WEST BROMPTON · FULHAM ROAD · KINGS ROAD · CHELSEA · CHELSEA EMBANKMENT · RIVER THAMES · VAUXHALL · ALBERT EMBANKMENT

FULHAM · BATTERSEA PARK · BATTERSEA PARK RD · SOUTH LAMBETH

NICHOLSON COMPUTER MAPPING

Nicholson

An Imprint of Bartholomew
A Division of HarperCollinsPublishers

A Nicholson Guide

Nicholson an imprint of
Bartholomew a division of
HarperCollins*Publishers*

First published 1974
10th edition 1993

© Nicholson 1993

London Map
© Nicholson generated from the Bartholomew
London Digital Database

London Underground Map by
permission of London Regional Transport
LRT Registered User No 93/1496

Other maps © Nicholson

Nicholson
HarperCollins*Publishers*
77-85 Fulham Palace Road
Hammersmith
London W6 8JB

Great care has been taken throughout this book to be accurate,
but the publishers cannot accept responsibility for any errors which
appear, or their consequences.

Printed in Great Britain by
Scotprint Ltd, Musselburgh

ISBN 0 7028 2243 4

92/10/1615 ENM

SYMBOLS AND ABBREVIATIONS

A - Access/Mastercard/Eurocard
Ax - American Express
Dc - Diners Club
V - Visa/Barclaycard

Average prices for a three-course meal for one
without wine but including VAT:
£   - £10.00 or under
££   - £10.00-£20.00
£££   - £20.00-£30.00
£££+ - £30.00 and over

Reserve - advisable to reserve
B - breakfast
L - lunch
D - dinner
🍺 - open all day 11.00-23.00 Mon-Sat, 12.00-14.00 & 19.00-
     22.30 Sun
(M) - membership required

Opening times
Many places are closed on Xmas Day, New Year's Day and Good
Friday, and general opening times are subject to change, so it is
always advisable to check first.

CONTENTS

ESSENTIALS ON ARRIVAL

Arriving in London can be daunting as there is so much to take in. However, with essential information at your fingertips, it doesn't have to be an unpleasant experience. Here is useful information you may need from the outset, which will allow you to enjoy all the delights London has to offer.

From airports to the city

Gatwick Airport
West Sussex. (0293) 535353. **By train**: Gatwick Express (071-928 5100) to Victoria Station (**7 B2**). Trains take *30 mins* and run from *06.20-20.50 (every 15 mins), 21.20-23.50 (every 30 mins), 01.00-06.20 (every hour on the hour) Mon-Sun*. **By coach**: Flightline 777 (081-668 7261) to Victoria Bus Station (**7 B2**). Coaches take about *1¼ hours* (longer in heavy traffic) and depart Gatwick at *05.20, 06.50; then every hour until 22.00 Mon-Sun*. **By car**: M23/A23 to central London, *approx 1 hour*.

Heathrow Airport
Bath Rd, Heathrow, Middx. 081-759 4321. **By tube**: (Piccadilly line) *approx 50 mins* to Piccadilly Circus (**4 E3**) and run from Heathrow *05.08-23.33 Mon-Sat, 06.40-22.46 Sun* and from Piccadilly Circus to Heathrow *05.46-24.21 Mon-Sat, 07.03-23.25 Sun*. **By bus**: (071-222 1234) A1 to Victoria Coach Station SW1 (**7 B2**) via Earl's Court, Gloucester Road, Knightsbridge and Hyde Park Corner. The bus takes about *1 hour* and runs from *06.40-20.00 (every 30 mins) Mon-Sun*. A2 to Woburn Pl WC1 (**1 G5**) via Holland Park, Notting Hill Gate, Queensway, Lancaster Gate and Paddington. The bus takes about *1¼-1½ hours* and runs from *06.00-22.00 (every 30 mins) Mon-Sun*. There is another bus service, Airbus (081-897 3305), to Victoria Coach Station (**7 B2**) *06.40-20.00 (every 30 mins) Mon-Sun*. **By car**: M4 to west London, *approx 30 mins*, but can take longer in heavy traffic.

London City Airport
King George V Dock, Silvertown E16. 071-474 5555. Mainly used by businessmen commuting to and from London for meetings. Flights go to Paris, Brussels, Rotterdam, Lille and

Jersey. **By rail**: British Rail from Silvertown to Stratford (Central line underground), then *45-min* journey to central London. **By boat**: Riverbus from Charing Cross Pier which connects with a minibus service from Canary Wharf to the airport. Journey takes *40 mins;* runs *every 20 mins between 07.15-19.45 Mon-Fri; every 30 mins between 10.30-16.30 Sat; and every 30 mins between 10.30-17.30 Sun.*

Luton Airport
Luton, Beds. (0582) 405100. **By train**: to King's Cross Station (on the Thameslink line) (**1 G3**) trains take about *40 mins* and run from *05.00-08.00 (every 20 mins), 08.00-20.00 (every 15 mins), 20.00-23.30 (every 30 mins) Mon-Sun; at 00.35 (Mon-Sun) & 03.23 (Mon-Fri)*. Connecting buses take passengers to the train station, but there are no night buses between *22.50-04.55 Mon-Fri, 23.20-04.55 Sat, 23.50-06.50 Sun;* passengers must take a taxi at these times.
By coach: to Victoria Bus Station (**7 B2**) coaches take about *1¼ hours* and run from *05.30-22.00 (every hour, except 21.00) Mon-Sun (from 06.00 Sat & Sun)*.

Stansted Airport
Stansted, Essex. (0279) 662380. **By train**: to Liverpool Street Station (**2 G6**) from Stansted Station (underneath the airport terminal) trains take *41 mins* and run *every 30 mins* from *06.00-23.00 Mon-Fri, 07.00-23.00 Sat, 07.30-23.00 Sun*. **By coach**: to Victoria (**7 B2**) the coach takes *1½ hours* and runs from Stansted *06.40-18.55 (every 2 hours) Mon-Sun* and from Victoria *09.00-21.00 Mon-Sun*.

Hotel booking agents

Accommodation Service of the London Tourist Board 7 B2
London Tourist Board Information Centre, Victoria Station Forecourt SW1. 071-730 3488. Information and bookings. *Open 09.00-20.30 Mon-Sun (to 22.00 Jul & Aug)*. Also at Heathrow Airport (Terminals 1,2 & 3). Personal callers only. *Open 08.00-18.00 Mon-Sun.* Charge.
Concordia Travel Hotel Reservations 7 B1
All kinds of hotels in London, Britain and worldwide. Sales desk at Victoria Station, opposite Platform 12. 071-828 4646. *Open 07.00-23.00 Mon-Sun.* Charge.
Hotel Booking Service 4 D3
4 New Burlington Place W1. 071-437 5052. Knowledgeable service on hotels in London, Britain and worldwide. *Open 09.30-17.30 Mon-Fri.* Free.
Hotel Reservations Centre 7 B2
10 Buckingham Palace Rd SW1. 071-828 2425. Bookings all over Britain. *Open 09.00-18.00 Mon-Fri.* Free.

Information centres

British Travel Centre   **4 D3**
12 Lower Regent St SW1. Personal callers only. British Tourist
Authority Information Centre, incorporating a British Rail ticket
office and a bureau de change. Book a room, a coach trip or
theatre ticket, buy plane or train tickets or hire a car. *Open
09.00-18.30 Mon-Fri, 10.00-16.00 Sat & Sun (09.00-17.30 Sat
in Jun-Sep only).*

City of London Information Centre   **5 D2**
St Paul's Churchyard EC4. 071-260 1456. Information and
advice with specific reference to the 'Square Mile'. Free
leaflets and literature available. *Open May-Sep 09.30-17.00
Mon-Sun; Oct-Apr 09.30-17.00 Mon-Fri, 09.30-12.30 Sat.*

London Tourist Board Information Centre   **7 B2**
Victoria Station Forecourt SW1. 071-730 3488. Travel and
tourist information for London and England. Most languages
spoken. Hotel reservations, theatre and tour bookings, guide
books and maps. *Open Apr-Oct 08.00-19.00 Mon-Sun;
Nov-Mar 08.00-19.00 Mon-Sat, 08.00-16.00 Sun. Telephone
service 09.00-18.00 Mon-Fri all year.*

Other London Tourist Board information centres at:
Heathrow Central Underground Station
Selfridges, 400 Oxford St W1.   **4 B2**

London Transport Travel Information Centre   **4 E6**
55 Broadway SW1. 071-222 1234. They will answer queries
about buses and the underground. Free maps of the bus and
underground routes, plus information leaflets in French,
German and English are available. *Opening times of the information centre vary; phone for details. Telephone information
service 24 hrs. Automatic telephone call queueing system.*

**Other London Transport travel information centres at the
following underground stations:**
Euston   **1 F4**
Heathrow
King's Cross   **1 G3**
Oxford Circus   **4 D2**
Piccadilly Circus   **4 E3**
Victoria (British Rail station)   **7 B2**

Scottish Tourist Board   **4 E4**
19 Cockspur St SW1. 071-930 8661. Tourist information on
mainland Scotland and the islands. *Open for leaflets and information May-Sep 09.00-18.00 Mon-Fri (to 18.30 Thur), 10.00-
16.00 Sat (Jun-Aug only); Oct-Apr 09.30-17.30 Mon-Fri (to
18.30 Thur). Open 09.30-17.00 Mon-Fri all year for bookings.*

Wales Information Bureau   **4 D3**
12 Lower Regent St W1. 071-409 0969. Leaflets and informa-

tion for the visitor to Wales. *Open 09.00-18.30 Mon-Fri, 10.00-16.00 Sat & Sun (09.00-17.30 Sat in Jun-Sep only).*

On the move

London has a comprehensive system of public transport with three different services – the bus, the underground (tube) and British Rail overground trains. It is one of the busiest in Europe, but if you take time to work out your route carefully it can give an excellent dimension on London life.

For the latest update on the travel situation call **Travel Check** *(24 hrs) on 071-222 1200.*

The majority of public transport services in London make no provision for disabled passengers. Consult Nicholson's Access in London *for advice on getting around.*

THE UNDERGROUND

Commonly known as the 'tube', for the visitor to London this is the simplest way of getting around. Very efficient in central London and a good service to north London, although few lines run south of the river, where British Rail offers a more comprehensive service. The tubes run between *approx 05.30-00.15 Mon-Sat, 07.30-23.30 Sun.* All tube stations have a notice showing the times of first and last trains and timetables are issued free at Travel Information Centres (see page 20). **Fares** are graduated according to zones. Travelcards, giving unlimited travel for one day, a week, a month or a year provide considerable savings. Travelcards can be used on the underground, DLR and buses, and can be bought at any tube station. Keep some 5p, 10p, 20p and £1 coins handy to use in the ticket machines. Cheap day returns are available after *09.30 Mon-Fri* or *any time Sat & Sun.* Keep your ticket to use in the exit machine at your destination. **Smoking** is illegal anywhere on the underground, including in the ticket halls, on stairs, escalators and platforms, as well as in the trains.

Docklands Light Railway (DLR)

Opened in 1987 to serve the 'new city' of Docklands. It runs from Bank or Tower Gateway (near Tower Hill) to Island Gardens (opposite Greenwich on the Isle of Dogs) or Stratford. The red, white and blue trains are computer-operated, although they do have a guard/ticket collector on board. There are excellent views from their high viaduct route over the stretches of water which form the Docklands. Trains run between *05.30-21.30 Mon-Fri. NB: No service Sat & Sun.*

BUSES

Covering the whole of Greater London, the famous red, double-decker buses, with the open platform at the back, are the best way to see London, but they are slower than the tubes, especially in the rush hours *(between 08.00-09.30 & 16.30-18.00 Mon-Fri)*. They run from *approx 06.00-24.00 Mon-Sat, 07.30-23.30 Sun*. First and last times of bus routes are indicated on bus stops, but traffic can prevent buses from keeping to these times. Buses stop automatically at compulsory bus stops (white background with a red horizontal line through a red circle). At a request stop (red background with a white horizontal line through a white circle) you must raise or wave your arm to hail the bus, and if you want to get off at a request stop, you must ring the bell once, in good time. On driver-only buses, the bells are on the silver hand rails. On open platform buses, pull the cord overhead downstairs, and push the button at the top of the stairs upstairs. *Fares* are graduated according to zones. The open-platform buses have a conductor who will collect your fare once the bus is moving. The newer buses have only a driver who you must pay as you board the bus. Both give change but do not like being given notes. Keep your ticket until you get off.

Nightbuses run through central London from about *23.00-06.00*. All pass through Trafalgar Square. Consult *Buses for Night Owls* for timetables, available from London Transport travel information centres (see page 20). Travelcards (except for one-day Travelcards) can be used on nightbuses.

BRITISH RAIL TRAINS

British Rail run InterCity trains all over Britain, and also Network SouthEast, which serves London and the suburbs. Most routes interchange with the underground – timetables are available from the British Travel Centre (see page 20) and from British Rail stations. These trains generally run *06.00-24.00 Mon-Sat, 07.00-22.30 Sun*. *Fares* are graduated and cheap day returns are available except during the rush hours *(08.00-09.30 & 16.30-18.00 Mon-Fri)*; you can also use Travelcards. The Thameslink service gets through London quickly, and goes from Luton Airport via West Hampstead and Blackfriars to Gatwick Airport, Brighton and Kent. Ask at any British Rail station for a timetable.The main British Rail terminals are:

Blackfriars   **5 C3**
Queen Victoria St EC4. Enquiries: 071-928 5100. Trains to south and south-east London suburbs.

Cannon Street   **5 E3**
Cannon St EC4. Enquiries: 071-928 5100. Trains to south-east London suburbs, Kent and East Sussex.

Charing Cross   **4 F4**
Strand WC2. Enquiries: 071-928 5100. Trains to south-east London suburbs and Kent.

Euston   **1 F4**
Euston Rd NW1. Enquiries: 071-387 7070. Trains to the

Midlands, northern England and Scotland.
Fenchurch Street 5 F3
Railway Place, Fenchurch St EC3. Enquiries: 071-928 5100.
Trains to Essex.
King's Cross 1 G3
Euston Rd N1. Enquiries: 071-278 2477. Trains to north-east
London suburbs, the Midlands, northern England and
Scotland.
Liverpool Street 5 F1
Liverpool St EC2. Enquiries: 071-928 5100. Trains to east and
north-east London suburbs, Cambridge and East Anglia.
London Bridge 5 E4
Borough High St SE1. Enquiries: 071-928 5100. Trains to
south-east London suburbs, Kent, Sussex and Surrey.
Marylebone 1 B5
Boston Place NW1. Enquiries: 071-262 6767. Trains to west
and north-west London suburbs and Buckinghamshire.
Moorgate 5 E1
Moorgate EC2. Enquiries: 071-278 2477. Trains to north
London suburbs and Hertfordshire.
Paddington 3 E2
Praed St W2. Enquiries: 071-262 6767. Trains to west and
south-west England and Wales.
St Pancras 2 A4
Euston Rd NW1. Enquiries: 071-387 7070. Trains to the
Midlands, north-west England and north-west London suburbs.
Victoria 7 B2
Terminus Place, Victoria St SW1. Enquiries: 071-928-5100.
Trains to south and south-east London suburbs.
Waterloo 5 B5
York Rd SE1. Enquiries: 071-928 5100. Trains to south-west
London suburbs, west Surrey, and the south coast of England.

GREEN LINE COACHES
These are express buses run by London Country. Most run
from central London to outlying areas within a 40-mile (64km)
radius. Main departure point is Eccleston Bridge SW1 (**7 B2**),
but there is another departure point on Regent Street just
north of Oxford Circus (**4 D2**). For information on schedules
and fares phone 081-668 7261.

RIVERBUS
The riverbus travels between Chelsea Harbour Pier and
Greenwich Pier *(50 minute journey) every 20 minutes
between 07.00-20.00 Mon-Fri and every 30 minutes between
11.00-16.30 Sat & Sun.* It travels via:
Cadogan Pier
Charing Cross Pier (Embankment) 4 G4
Festival Pier (The South Bank Centre) 4 G4

Swan Lane Pier (The City)   **5 E3**
London Bridge City Pier   **5 F4**
St Katharine's Pier
West India Pier (Docklands & Canary Wharf)
The riverbus from Charing Cross Pier now connects with a minibus service from Canary Wharf to London City Airport. For details of this service see page 19. For further information on Riverbus services phone 071-987 0311.

TAXIS

The famous London black taxi cabs, which can now also be red, blue, green or even white (!) can be hailed in the street. A taxi is available for hire if the yellow 'taxi' sign above the windscreen is lit. If the driver stops, s/he is obliged to take you wherever you want to go, provided the destination is no more than 6 miles (9.6km) – otherwise it is at their discretion. All taxis have meters which the driver must use on all journeys within the Metropolitan Police District (most of Greater London and to Heathrow). For longer journeys the price should be negotiated with the driver beforehand. There is a minimum payable charge which is shown on the meter when you hire a cab. Expect to pay extra for large amounts of luggage, journeys between *20.00-06.00, at weekends and Bank hols*. You can order a black cab by telephone *24 hrs* a day, but this will be more expensive than hailing one in the street as you will be charged for being picked up as well as taken to your destination.
Computer-cab: 071-286 0286.
Dial-a-Cab: 071-253 5000.
Ladycabs: 071-254 3501. Late night cabs for women, driven by women. Operate *to 00.30 Mon-Thur, to 01.00 Fri, to 02.00 Sat, to 24.00 Sun*.
Radio Taxicabs: 071-272 0272.

MINICABS

These cannot be hailed in the street, and are indistinguishable from private cars. Unlike black cabs, they are not licensed, nor do their drivers take the same stringent test. The cars have no meters, so it is essential to negotiate the price of each journey in advance. They are usually cheaper than black cabs over long distances, especially *at night and weekends*. Look in the *Yellow Pages* for lists of minicab companies.

Telephone services

ESSENTIAL NUMBERS
999: Emergency (Ambulance, Police, Fire)
100: Operator

155: International operator
142/192: Directory enquiries (142 – London, 192 – national)
153: International directory enquiries
123: Speaking clock
Telegrams: dial 100 and ask for International Telegrams (must be a day in advance).

TO FIND A NUMBER
London residential directories are in two volumes covering the alphabet from A-Z. The business directory covers A-Z in one volume. In addition, *Yellow Pages* covers all businesses in London listed alphabetically by trade (volumes by region). For directory enquiries (for which there is a charge unless you are calling from a public telephone box) you should have the name and address of the person/company you wish to contact.

MAKING A CALL
London numbers have now been prefixed with 081- and 071- instead of the previous 01-. Generally central London numbers are 071- and Greater London are 081-. If you are not sure which to dial, telephone the operator (100 – free) and they will tell you. It is not necessary to use the prefix when dialling within a zone. The *Code Book* lists all exchanges outside London (or the operator will tell you) including international numbers.

PUBLIC TELEPHONES
The old red telephone boxes have now almost entirely disappeared, to be replaced by glass constructions. They are usually to be found in groups around stations (tube and train), in hotels, pubs and public places. There are several types:
Coin-operated which take 5p, 10p, 20p, 50p and £1 coins (minimum charge 10p); coins must be inserted before you can dial, but if you do not get through the money will be refunded (it is best to use smaller denominations as percentages of larger ones will not be refunded).
Phonecard which accept only British Telecom phonecards, obtainable from newsagents, chemists, post offices etc, and in denominations from 20 units (£2.00) to 200 units (£20.00).
Mercury phonecard which accept only Mercury phonecards, obtainable from newsagents, chemists, post offices etc, or credit cards – A.Ax.Dc.V. (minimum charge 50p).

COSTS
These are assessed according to time of day, distance and length of call. There are three different rates: ***Peak***: *09.00-13.00 Mon-Fri,* ***Standard***: *08.00-09.00 & 13.00-18.00 Mon-Fri* and ***Cheap***: *18.00-08.00 Mon-Fri & all day and night Sat & Sun.* Cheap time for most international calls is *18.00-08.00.*

Money

CURRENCY
The unit of currency in Britain is the pound sterling (£) divided into 100 pence (p). There are coins for 1p, 2p, 5p, 10p, 20p, 50p and £1, with notes for £5, £10, £20 and £50.

EXCHANGE FACILITIES
There is no exchange control in Britain, so you can carry any amount of money through customs, in or out of the country. The best rate of exchange is always to be found in a bank. Bureaux de change will exchange most currencies and will cash cheques, but charge more. They can be found at airports, main-line train stations, central tube stations and in the larger department stores. They operate outside banking hours. Most large hotels will accept travellers' cheques in payment of bills.

Chequepoint Bureau de Change

222 Earl's Court Rd SW5. 071-373 9515.	**6 A2**
Marble Arch, 548 Oxford St W1. 071-723 2646.	**4 A3**

Eurochange Bureau

95 Buckingham Palace Rd SW1. 071-834 3330.	**7 B2**
45 Charing Cross Rd WC2. 071-439 2827.	**4 F3**
Paddington Tube Station W2. 071-258 0442.	**3 E2**

Thomas Cook

104 Kensington High St W8. 071-376 2588.	**3 B6**
100 Victoria St SW1. 071-828 8985.	**7 C1**
Selfridges, 400 Oxford St W1. 071-629 1234.	**4 B2**

BANKS
Standard banking hours are *09.30-15.30 Mon-Fri* although many branches are now open *until 16.30 Mon-Fri and on Sat morning.* They are closed on *Bank holidays* and often close early the *day before a Bank holiday.*

TIPPING
Should be an expression of pleasure for service rendered and never a duty. It is possible not to tip at all if the circumstances justify this. These guidelines give some idea of the average tip:

Restaurants Many add on a service charge, usually 12½%, but do not always say so – if in doubt, ask them. They usually say if it is *not* included.

Taxis 10-15%

Commissionaires for getting a taxi. Up to £1 depending on the effort expended.

Pubs & bars Never at the bar, but buy the barman a drink if you wish. For waiter service in the lounge, from 20p per drink.

Hotels Almost all add it to your bill, usually 10%. Give extra to individuals for special service, from 50p.
Porters 50p-£1 per case depending on how far it is carried.

Car hire

*The law now states that **all** occupants of a car must wear safety belts. This includes the driver, and all passengers (although it only applies to back seat passengers if safety belts have already been fitted). **Don't** park on double yellow lines; it will result in a parking fine or wheelclamp (both are expensive).*
To hire a car you will normally need to be over 21 and to have held a licence, valid for use in the UK, for at least a year. Overseas visitors' licences are valid in Britain for a year. Prices differ greatly from company to company and depend on the make of car and the season. There is a basic daily, weekly or monthly charge and you will be required to leave a deposit.

Avis 4 B2
8 Balderton St W1. 071-245 9862. You can book a car for anywhere in London from here. *Open 07.30-19.30 Mon-Sun.* Worldwide reservations: 081-848 8733.

EuroDollar
Swan National House, Warwick Place, Uxbridge, Middx. (0895) 233300. Book for London or worldwide from this office. *Open 08.00-18.00 Mon-Fri, to 13.00 Sat.*

Hertz Rent-a-Car
Radnor House, 1272 London Rd SW16. 081-679 1799. Branches throughout London, Britain and the Continent. *Open 08.00-18.00 Mon-Fri, to 17.00 Sat.*

Bicycle hire

The bike offers an alternative and often more interesting form of transport. London has become far more geared to cyclists in recent years and there are now special cycle lanes on many roads. Danger to health from noxious fumes is not nearly as great as the benefit gained from the exercise of cycling. Explore streets, relax in parks and avoid parking difficulties!

London Bicycle Tours 5 B4
56 Upper Ground SE1. 071-928 6838. Bicycle hire; also organises tours. *Open Easter-Oct. Phone for details.*

On Your Bike 5 E4
22 Duke Street Hill SE1. 071-357 6958. *Open 09.00-18.00 Mon-Fri, 09.30-17.00 Sat.*

Portobello Cycles
69 Golborne Rd W10. 081-960 0444. *Open 10.00-17.00 Mon-Sat.*

HISTORIC LONDON

London's history begins in AD43, when invading Romans bridged the Thames. They built the London Wall around AD200, traces of which are still visible today. This was to determine the shape of what is still called the City of London for some 1300 years. Despite the devastation of three-fifths of the City during the Great Fire of 1666, no radical replanning took place immediately within the 'Square Mile'. However, a massive scheme grew out of the ashes beyond the City which was to create the London we know today. Surrounding villages were absorbed and now give their names to central districts of the capital.

London's growth resulted from rising commercial importance (the City is still one of the world's major financial centres), the Industrial Revolution, and more recently, developing public transport which pushed new suburbs well out into the countryside.

London has, naturally, changed enormously through the years, but, despite the Blitz and decades of redevelopment, every stage of London's history can be traced through her buildings, monuments, churches and famous houses.

Historic sights and buildings

Admiralty Arch   4 E4
Entrance to the Mall SW1. Massive Edwardian triple arch by Sir Aston Webb 1911. A memorial to Queen Victoria.

Albert Memorial   3 E5
Kensington Gore SW7. Gothic memorial to Queen Victoria's consort, Prince Albert, by Sir George Gilbert Scott, 1872. It is 175ft (53.3m) high with a 14ft (4.3m) statue of the Prince by John Foley.

Apsley House   4 B5
149 Piccadilly W1. 071-499 5676. Originally known as 'Number One London', home of the 1st Duke of Wellington. Robert Adam 1778, alterations by Wyatt 1828. Now a museum. *Closed for restoration at time of publication.*

BBC Broadcasting House   1 D6
Portland Place W1. 071-580 4468. G. Val Myers 1928. Imposing headquarters of the British Broadcasting Corporation where the Director-General and Governors meet to discuss the BBC's broadcasting policy.

Bank of England **5 E2**
Threadneedle St EC2. 071-601 5545. The government and bankers' bank and custodian of the nation's gold reserves. Outer walls are the original design of Sir John Soane, architect to the Bank 1788-1833. Interior redesigned by Sir Herbert Baker 1925-39. Museum (see page 53) *open to the public.*

Banqueting House **4 F4**
Whitehall SW1. 071-930 4179. Inigo Jones 1619-25. Only surviving part of Whitehall Palace, used for state and court ceremonies. *Open 10.00-17.00 Mon-Sat.* Charge.

Barbican **5 C1**
Silk St EC2. 071-638 4141. Chamberlin, Powell and Bon 1955. Over 2000 apartments (some the highest in Europe when built), a water garden, the restored St Giles Cripplegate Church, a girls' school, pubs, shops, a museum and the Barbican Centre (1982) – the largest arts centre in the country. *Open 10.00-20.00 Mon-Sun.*

British Telecom Tower **1 E6**
Maple St W1. 071-580 6767. Eric Bedford 1966. Stands 580ft (176.7m) high topped by a 39ft (11.9m) mast with radar aerial. Houses telecommunications equipment and offices. *Closed to the public.*

Buckingham Palace **4 D5**
St James's Park SW1. 071-930 4832. The official London residence of the Queen. Built 1705, enlarged 1825 by Nash. 600 rooms, 12 occupied by Queen Elizabeth II and the Duke of Edinburgh. The Royal Standard is flown when the Queen is in residence.

Burlington Arcade **4 D3**
Piccadilly W1. 1819 Regency arcade famous for small, exclusive shops. Beadles still ensure obedience to rules forbidding 'singing, carrying large parcels, and running'!

Canary Wharf Tower
West India Docks, Isle of Dogs E14. Tallest building in the United Kingdom, 800ft (244m) high, set in an 80-acre (35ha) 'new district' with shops, offices, apartments, restaurants and waterfront promenades.

Carnaby Street **4 D3**
W1. The first men's boutique opened in 1957. World famous by the 1960s and the heart of fashion during the following swinging decade, especially for pop stars. Still has a lively, if not so fashionable, image.

The Cenotaph **4 F5**
Whitehall SW1. Sir Edwin Lutyens (1920) to honour the dead of the First World War, and now those who died in both World Wars. The word comes from the Greek *kenos* meaning empty and *taphos* meaning tomb. The annual Service of Remembrance takes place here in *November* (see page 52).

Chelsea Royal Hospital   7 A3
Royal Hospital Rd SW3. 071-730 0161. Established 1682 by Charles II for veteran soldiers. Designed by Wren and opened in 1689 admitting 476 army pensioners. Fine carvings, several royal portraits and a museum. *Open 10.00-12.00 & 14.00-16.30 Mon-Sat, 14.00-16.00 Sun (closed Sun in winter).* Free.

Clarence House   4 D5
Stable Yard Gate SW1. Elegant stuccoed mansion by Nash 1825. Now home of the Queen Mother. *Closed to the public.*

Cleopatra's Needle   5 A3
Victoria Embankment SW1. Brought from Heliopolis, dates to 1500 BC. Presented by Egypt and erected here 1878.

Covent Garden   4 F3
WC2. Originally designed by Inigo Jones as a residential square in the 1630s. Market buildings by Fowler 1830; Floral Hall added 1860 by E.M. Barry, architect of the Royal Opera House (1858). In 1974 the flower market moved to Nine Elms (**7 D5**), but the area survived to become a flourishing new community with an eclectic, though expensive, range of shops and places to eat and drink.

Docklands
The once prosperous London docks fell into decline in the 1960s as sea traffic moved downstream to Tilbury. New development began in the the mid-1980s and continues unabated. Neglected wharves have been given a new lease of life, with St Katharine's Dock (**5 G3**) the first to be converted into shops, restaurants and a hotel. Other areas worth exploring are Tobacco Dock, and West India Docks on the Isle of Dogs.

Downing Street   4 F5
SW1. Built by Sir George Downing MP in 17thC. No.10 is the official residence of the Prime Minister; No.11 that of the Chancellor of the Exchequer; and No.12 is the Party Whips' Office. *Wrought-iron gates prevent direct public access.*

Fleet Street   5 B2
EC4. London's 'Street of Ink', associated with printing since Caxton, has now lost most of its newspapers as new technology moved them elsewhere. Connections still remain.

Greenwich
Cutty Sark
King William Walk SE10. 081-858 3445. One of the great tea clippers, built 1869, now in dry dock. Explore the galley and cabins. Next to it is *Gipsy Moth IV*, in which Sir Francis Chichester sailed single-handed round the world in 1966. Both *open Apr-Sep 10.00-17.30 Mon-Sat, 12.00-17.30 Sun; Oct-Mar 10.00-16.30 Mon-Sat, 12.00-16.30 Sun.* Charge.

Museum of Artillery
The Rotunda, Repository Rd, Woolwich Common SE18. 081-

854 2242 x 3128. Pavilion by Nash, 1822. A renowned collection of guns and muskets, rifles, armour and early rockets from France, Burma, Britain and India. *Open 12.30-16.30 Mon-Fri, 14.00-16.00 Sat & Sun*. Voluntary donation.

Old Royal Observatory
Greenwich Park SE10. 081-858 1167. Part of the National Maritime Museum. Founded by Charles II in 1675 and designed by Wren. Stand astride the Meridian line to be in both the eastern and western hemispheres at the same time. Extensive collection of time-measuring instruments. *Open Apr-Sep 10.00-18.00 Mon-Sat, 14.00-18.00 Sun; Oct-Mar 10.00-17.00 Mon-Sat, 14.00-17.00 Sun*. Charge.

Royal Naval College
Greenwich SE10. 081-858 2154. On the site of Greenwich Palace, Wren's beautiful baroque building, 1694, houses Sir James Thornhill's amazing Painted Hall (which took 20 years to complete). *Open 14.30-16.45 Mon-Sun (closed Thur)*. Free.

Guildhall   5 D2
Off Gresham St EC2. 071-606 3030. Built 1411-40 with alterations by George Dance 1789 and Sir Giles Gilbert Scott 1953. Great Hall used for ceremonial occasions – there was a banquet here to celebrate Queen Elizabeth II's coronation. Library established 1423. Medieval crypt the most extensive of its kind in London. Great Hall *open 09.00-17.30 Mon-Sat*. Free. Library *open 09.30-17.00 Mon-Sat*. Free. The Museum of the Clockmakers Company is contained within the library and is *open 09.30-16.45 Mon-Fri*. Free.

Hampton Court Palace
Hampton Court, East Molesey, Surrey. 081-977 8441. Riverside Tudor palace built 1514 for Cardinal Wolsey and acquired by Henry VIII who greatly enlarged it. Later additions by Wren in the 1690s for William III and Mary. Sumptuous state rooms decorated by Vanbrugh, Verrio and Thornhill. Famous picture gallery of Italian masterpieces, the Orangery, the Great Vine and the Maze. Spectacular formal gardens. *Open mid Mar-Oct 10.15-18.00 Mon, 09.30-18.00 Tue-Sun; Nov-mid Mar 10.15-16.30 Mon, 09.30-16.30 Tue-Sun*. Charge.

Houses of Parliament   4 F6
St Margaret St SW1. 071-219 3000. Originally the Palace of Westminster and a principal royal palace until 1512. Became known as 'parliament' or 'place to speak' in 1550. Westminster Hall, one of the few remaining parts of the original palace, has an impressive hammerbeam roof. The present Victorian Gothic building was designed in 1847 by Sir Charles Barry and Augustus Pugin specifically to house Parliament and has over 1100 rooms, 100 staircases and over 2 miles (3.2 km)

of passages. Recently cleaned to reveal their full architectural beauty, the Houses of Parliament and Big Ben – the bell clock housed in the adjoining St Stephen's Tower – make up London's most famous landmark. *To arrange a visit or tour contact your local MP for advance tickets to the Visitors' Gallery or queue at St Stephen's entrance (there are very long queues in summer; advisable to go after 17.00 to avoid them). No small children allowed.* Free.

Hyde Park Corner   4 B5
SW1. Constitution Arch and the Ionic Screen of three classical-style triumphal arches by Decimus Burton 1825. Once intended as an imposing and pleasing feature of the journey from Buckingham Palace to Hyde Park, it now swarms with traffic and underground pedestrians.

Inns of Court
Four great Inns of Court, dating from the 14thC, which act as a law school and have the exclusive privilege of calling candidates to the English Bar. Before they are eligible to be called, prospective barristers must pass the Bar exams, join one of the four Inns of Court and dine 24 times in the halls.

Gray's Inn   5 B1
Holborn WC1 (entrance from passage next to 22 High Holborn). 071-405 8164. An Inn of Court since the 14thC, although the oldest surviving buildings are 17thC. Francis Bacon had chambers here from 1577 until his death. He reportedly laid out the gardens and planted the Catalpa trees.

Lincoln's Inn   5 A2
Chancery Lane WC2. 071-405 1393. Parts of Lincoln's Inn date back to the 13thC, and it still has a Dickensian atmosphere. Famous members include Disraeli, Gladstone and Oliver Cromwell. *Open 10.00-16.00 Mon-Fri (gardens open 12.00-14.30 only). Closed Sat & Sun. Admission to the chapel outside these hours and to the Hall and Library by application to the Treasury Office, Whitehall SW1.* Free.

Inner Temple   5 B2
Crown Office Row EC4. 071-797 8250. The Inner Temple dates from 1505. Prince Henry's Room, above the Gateway (1610), is the oldest domestic building in London and home to the Samuel Pepys Club and Pepysian memorabilia. *Open 10.00-16.00 Mon-Fri by arrangement. Closed Sat, Sun, Bank hols & legal vacations.*

Middle Temple   5 B3
Middle Temple Lane EC4. 071-353 4355. Dates from 1570. Together with the Inner Temple it comprises courtyards, alleys, gardens and warm brick buildings. *Open 10.00-12.00 & 15.00-16.00 (by arrangement) Mon-Fri. Closed Sat, Sun, Bank hols, Aug & during examinations.* Free.

Jewel Tower **4 F6**
Old Palace Yard SW1. 071-222 2219. 14thC surviving frag-
ment of the Palace of Westminster, once the safe for Edward
III's jewels, clothes and furs, now home to a collection of
objects found during excavations of the area. *Open Easter-Sep
10.00-13.00 & 14.00-18.00 Mon-Sun; Oct-Easter 10.00-13.00
& 14.00-16.00 Tue-Sun.* Charge.

Kensington Palace **3 C4**
Kensington Gardens W8. 071-937 9561. Bought by William III
and altered by the architects Christopher Wren and William
Kent. Orangery House by Hawksmoor and Vanbrugh for
Queen Anne in 1704. Queen Victoria was born here.
Apartments still used by members of the royal family. State
apartments *open 09.00-17.00 Mon-Sat, 11.00-17.00 Sun (last
admission 16.15). Closed Bank hols.* Charge.

Kenwood House (Iveagh Bequest)
Hampstead Lane NW3. 081-348 1286. Robert Adam 1764-9.
Edward Guinness, 1st Earl of Iveagh's collection of paintings
including works by van Dyck, Reynolds, Rembrandt,
Gainsborough and Turner. Gardens and wooded estate of 200
acres (81ha). *Open Easter-Sep 10.00-18.00 Mon-Sun; Oct-
Easter 10.00-16.00 Mon-Sun.* Free.

Lambeth Palace **7 F1**
Lambeth Palace Rd SE1. 071-928 8282. Official London
residence of the Archbishop of Canterbury since 1197.
13thC crypt beneath the chapel and Tudor gatehouse. The
gloves worn by Charles I when he went to the scaffold are
displayed along with a brass plate commemorating the neg-
ligence of the gardener who stuck his fork through
Archbishop Laud's tortoise. *Tours (very restricted) Wed or
Thur by written application to the Booking Secretary.*
Charge.

Law Courts **5 B2**
Strand WC2. 071-936 6000. Massive Victorian-Gothic building
housing the Royal Courts of Justice. More than 1000 rooms
and 3½ miles of corridor. *Open to public 09.00-17.00 Mon-Fri.*
Over 16s only. Courts not in session *Aug & Sep but still open
to the public.* Free.

Lloyds of London **5 F2**
Lime St EC3. 071-327 6210. Impressive glass and aluminium
structure by the Richard Rogers Partnership (jointly responsible
for the Pompidou Centre in Paris). Spectacular at night, this
multi-faceted, 12-storey structure is the headquarters for the
international insurance market. Huge dealing room in a 246ft
(75m) high atrium housing the famous Lutine Bell. Viewing
gallery *open to pre-booked groups only; to arrange group tours
of gallery phone above number.*

London Wall   5 D1
EC2. Parts of the old Roman wall still survive at St Alphage
Garden, St Giles Churchyard, Cripplegate St EC1 (**5 D1**); Jewry
St EC3 (**5 G2**); off Trinity Square EC3 (**5 F3**); and in the Tower
of London EC3 (**5 G3**).

Mansion House   5 E2
Walbrook EC4. 071-626 2500. Official residence of the Lord
Mayor of London, built 1739 by George Dance the Elder.
Palladian mansion with majestic Ball Room, Banqueting Room
and Egyptian Hall, lavishly decorated in 23-carat gold. *Closed
for renovation at time of publication.*

Marble Arch   3 G3
W1. John Nash 1827, based on the Arch of Constantine in
Rome. Only senior members of the Royal Family and the
King's Troop Royal Horse Artillery may pass through it.

Monument   5 E3
Monument St EC3. 071-626 2717. Wren 1671-7. Made of
Portland stone, it commemorates the Great Fire of 1666 and
stands at 202ft (61.5m), a foot in height for every foot in
distance from where the fire started in Pudding Lane. Summit
311 steps up spiral staircase. Magnificent views. *Open Apr-
Sep 09.00-17.40 Mon-Fri, 14.00-17.40 Sat & Sun; Oct-Mar
09.00-15.40 Mon-Sat. Charge. Due to close in 1993 for renovations. Phone for details.*

NatWest Tower   5 F2
Bishopsgate EC2. 1980. 600ft (183m) tower – tallest building
in Britain until the Canary Wharf Tower was completed in
1990 (see page 29). Slender, shining structure with a curious
pin-striped effect from the closeness of its vertical lines.
Dominates City skyline and houses the head office of the
National Westminster Bank.

Nelson's Column   4 E4
Trafalgar Sq WC2. By William Railton 1839-42, 145ft (44m)
column surmounted by a 16ft (5m) stone statue of Admiral
Lord Nelson by E.H. Baily, erected 1843. The statue is minus
his eye and arm, both lost in battle.

Old Bailey   5 C2
Old Bailey EC4. 071-248 3277. Central Criminal Court, on the
site of the old Newgate Prison. The scene for many famous
trials – Oscar Wilde in 1895, Dr Crippen in 1910, J.R. Christie
in 1953 and Peter Sutcliffe, 'the Yorkshire Ripper', in 1981.
Public viewing gallery. *Open 10.30-13.00 & 14.00-16.00 Mon-
Fri. Minimum age 14 (must be accompanied by an adult if
under 16). Free.*

Pall Mall   4 D4
SW1. Early 19thC opulence. Gentlemen's clubs were
established on this street as exclusive havens for their mem-

bers. Reform Club (No.104) by Charles Barry, from where the fictitious character Phileas Fogg began his trip *Around the World in 80 Days;* Travellers' Club (No.106) founded 1819; Athenaeum Club (No.107) founded for the intellectually elite.

Piccadilly Circus   **4 E3**

W1. The confluence of five major thoroughfares – Regent Street, Shaftesbury Avenue, Haymarket, Piccadilly and Lower Regent Street. Fountain and statue of Eros by Gilbert (1893). The world-famous neon advertising hoardings make it a far cry from its original elegant designs. The first, for Bovril and Schweppes at the turn of the century, caused a great scandal.

Regent Street   **4 D3**

John Nash, asked by George IV (then Prince of Wales) to construct a link from Carlton House (now demolished) to the royal country home near Regent's Park, not only designed the route for Regent Street but also most of the buildings along it. This took many years since it was pieced together to conform with various architectural styles along the way. Initially acclaimed, its imminent destruction was celebrated in 1927 when George V and his Queen drove down its flower-decked length – it was then rebuilt from end to end.

Ritz Hotel   **4 D4**

Piccadilly W1. 071-493 8181. Designed by César Ritz 1906. Archways based on the rue de Rivoli in Paris, interior in Louis XVI style.

Royal Albert Hall   **3 E5**

Kensington Gore SW7. 071-589 8212. Originally built as the 'Hall of Arts & Sciences', prefixed with 'Royal Albert' at the last minute by Queen Victoria. Oval, not circular, as you might imagine, this is the venue for a wide variety of events from organ recitals to boxing matches.

Royal Exchange   **5 E2**

cnr Threadneedle St & Cornhill EC3. Present building (the third) 1844 by Sir William Tite. Original destroyed in the Great Fire. Since 1982 home to the London International Financial Futures Exchange (LIFFE). More than 20,000 contracts are exchanged per day here. Watch the dealers in action. *Pre-booked tours only. Phone 071-623 0444 for details. Free.*

St James's Palace   **4 D4**

Pall Mall SW1. Built by Henry VIII for Anne Boleyn and used as a royal palace for over 300 years. Still a royal residence; no members of the royal family live there at present. Foreign ambassadors and High Commissioners are still accredited to the Court of St James although actually received at Buckingham Palace. Courtyards only *open to the public.*

Savile Row   **4 D3**

W1. World-famous as the headquarters of the finest of

London's tailors. Built 1730s as a residential street, it became fashionable amongst tailors from the mid-19thC.

Savoy Hotel   4 G3
Strand WC2. Richard D'Oyly Carte 1889. Impeccable and impressive standards. Monet painted Waterloo Bridge from its terraces. Still the favourite of the famous.

Soho   4 D2
An area bounded by Regent Street, Oxford Street, Shaftesbury Avenue and Charing Cross Road. Lively and notorious but perfectly safe, except for a handful of peep shows and strip joints. Narrow 18th and 19thC streets full of fascinating foreign food shops, restaurants, street markets, flashing neon and nightlife. Chinatown radiates from Gerrard Street.

Somerset House   4 G3
Strand WC2. On the site of an unfinished Renaissance palace (1547-50) with a history of many royal inhabitants. Present building by Sir William Chambers 1776. Once housed the register of births, marriages and deaths in England and Wales (see Public Record Office on page 58); now holds the register of divorce, wills and probate, offices of the Inland Revenue and the Courtauld Institute Galleries (see page 54). *Open 10.00-16.00 Mon-Fri.* Free.

Spitalfields   5 G1
E1. This centre of silk-weaving in England was established by the influx of Flemish and French weavers in the 16thC and 17thC. The industry reached its height at the end of the 18thC and early 19thC when about 17,000 looms were in use and a large area of East London was dependent on these family concerns. Fournier Street has some good examples of Dutch-style houses of the time. The industry collapsed some 100 years ago, but the streets here are still steeped in history and tradition.

Thames Barrier
Unity Way, Eastmoor St SE18. 081-854 1373. Steel fins form an impressive piece of modern engineering set up to stem dangerously high tides. Completed in 1982, it is the world's largest moveable flood barrier. The Visitor Centre houses an exhibition explaining the technology involved. *25-min* cruise from Barrier Pier *10.00-17.30 Sat, Sun & Bank hols.* Visitor Centre *open 10.00-17.00 Mon-Fri.* Charge.

Tower of London   5 G3
Tower Hill EC3. 071-709 0765. A keep, a prison and still a fortress, the Tower has served as a palace, place of execution and in its time has housed the Royal Mint, the Royal Observatory, the Royal Menagerie, and the Public Records. Now famous for the Bloody Tower, Traitors' Gate, the ravens, the Crown Jewels, the Armouries and the Yeomen Warders (or Beefeaters). British monarchs imprisoned here include

Edward III, Henry VII and Elizabeth I. Other prisoners have included Thomas More, Guy Fawkes and his fellow plotters, Sir Walter Raleigh, and Rudolf Hess, detained during World War II. Also the site of many executions including two of Henry VIII's wives – Anne Boleyn in 1536, and Catherine Howard in 1542, both of whom were given the privilege of a quiet execution on Tower Green. The Yeomen Warders still guard the Crown Jewels, with which the new monarch is invested at the coronation ceremony. *Open Mar-Oct 09.30-18.00 Mon-Sat, 10.00-18.00 Sun; Nov-Feb 09.30-17.00 Mon-Sat. Be prepared for long queues in summer.* Charge.

Trafalgar Square   **4 F4**
WC2. Laid out by Sir Charles Barry 1829. Nelson's column (see page 34) is surrounded by Landseer's four impressive bronze lions, 1868. Fountains by Lutyens. Famous for political rallies, pigeons and the excesses of New Year's Eve revellers.

Whitehall   **4 F4**
Wide thoroughfare once part of the ancient main route linking Westminster and the City, now used for ceremonial and State processions. Lined with Government offices including Old Admiralty, Old Scotland Yard, the War Office, the Foreign Office, Dover House, the Treasury, Horse Guards' Parade and Banqueting House.

Whittington Stone
Highgate Hill N6. Near the junction with Dartmouth Park Hill. The milestone marks the spot where tradition says Dick Whittington, London's most famous Lord Mayor, heard the Bow Bells chime 'Turn again, Whittington, thrice Lord Mayor of London'.

Houses of the famous

Carlyle's House   **6 E4**
24 Cheyne Row SW3. 071-352 7087. Modest Queen Anne terrace where Carlyle lived for 42 years until his death in 1881. Ruskin, Dickens and Kingsley were frequent visitors. *Open 11.00-17.00 (last admission 16.30) Wed-Sun & Bank hols except Good Fri. Closed Nov-Mar.* Charge.

Dickens' House   **2 B5**
48 Doughty St WC1. 071-405 2127. Regency terraced house where Charles Dickens and his family lived from 1837-9. Here he completed *The Pickwick Papers* and wrote *Oliver Twist* and *Nicholas Nickleby*. *Open 10.00-17.00 (last admission 16.30). Closed Sun & Bank hols.* Charge.

Freud Museum
20 Maresfield Gdns, Hampstead NW3. 071-435 2002. Exactly as it was when he died in 1939, the house in which Sigmund

Freud found refuge after fleeing Hitler in 1938. Extraordinary collection of Egyptian, Greek, Roman and Oriental antiquities and also the famous couch on which he conducted his analyses. *Open 12.00-17.00 Wed-Sun.* Charge.

Hogarth's House
Hogarth Lane, Great West Rd, Chiswick W4. 081-994 6757. William Hogarth's country retreat from 1749 until his death in 1764. Relics and impressions of his engravings on display. *Open Apr-Sep 11.00-18.00 Mon & Wed-Sat, 14.00-18.00 Sun; Oct-Mar 11.00-16.00 Mon & Wed-Sat, 14.00-16.00 Sun. Closed Tue, first two weeks of Sep & last three weeks of Dec.* Free.

Dr Johnson's House   5 B2
17 Gough Sq, Fleet St EC4. 071-353 3745. 17thC house in the attic of which Dr Samuel Johnson compiled his famous dictionary. Lived here from 1748-59. Relics include his chair from the Old Cock Tavern and a first edition of his dictionary. *Open May-Sep 11.00-17.30 Mon-Sat; Oct-Apr 11.00-17.00 Mon-Sat. Closed Sun & Bank hols.* Small charge.

Keats' House
Wentworth Place, Keats Grove, Hampstead NW3. 071-435 2062. The poet John Keats lived here from 1818-20, during which time his love affair with Fanny Brawne began. *Ode to a Nightingale* was composed in the garden in a single morning. *Open May-Oct 10.00-13.00 & 14.00-18.00 Mon-Fri, 10.00-13.00 & 14.00-17.00 Sat, 14.00-17.00 Sun; Nov-Apr 13.00-17.00 Mon-Fri, 10.00-13.00 & 14.00-17.00 Sat, 14.00-17.00 Sun.* Charge.

Leighton House   3 A6
12 Holland Park Rd W14. 071-602 3316. Eastern-style house, commissioned by Lord Frederick Leighton 1866. Arab Hall decorated with 14thC-16thC oriental tiles. Paintings by Leighton and Burne-Jones. Watts and De Morgan pottery. *Open 11.00-13.00 Mon-Sat. Closed Sun & Bank hols.* Free.

Wesley's House & Chapel   2 D3
47 City Rd EC1. 071-253 2262. Methodist John Wesley's possessions and personal relics, and his tomb in the nearby chapel. In the crypt a museum tells the story of Methodism. *Open 10.00-16.00 Mon-Sat, 12.00-14.00 Sun.* Small charge.

Places of worship

In their buildings, ruins, sites and associations, London's churches and cathedrals represent nearly 1400 years of Christianity in Britain. The Great Fire of 1666 set the scene for Wren's rebuilding programme, including St Paul's Cathedral and 50 other churches. The 17thC and early 18thC saw many more churches built, to the designs of Nicholas Hawksmoor and Inigo Jones, and the Victorians produced a wealth of new churches in the 19thC.

Non-Christian religions also have their part in London's history, with synagogues as at Bevis Marks and, most recently, the London Central Mosque in Regent's Park for London's growing Islamic community.

Entrance to all places of worship is free, unless otherwise stated.

All Souls, Langham Place   4 C1
Langham Place W1. 071-580 4357. Nash's only church, 1822-4. Unusual style – Corinthian columns and needle spire. Interior refitted 1976. Exterior restored 1987-8.

Bevis Marks Synagogue   5 F2
Heneage Lane (off Bevis Marks) EC3. 071-626 1274. Built in 1700, Britain's oldest surviving synagogue. Fine windows and brass chandeliers from Amsterdam.

Brompton Oratory   3 F6
Brompton Rd SW7. 071-589 4811. Baroque style, Herbert Gribble 1834. The centre of Roman Catholicism until Westminster Cathedral was built 1903. Ornate interior and fine statues, some originals from Cathedral of Siena.

Chapel Royal of St John   5 G3
White Tower, Tower of London EC3. 071-709 0765. The oldest Norman church in London, c1085. Original pillars still intact.

Chelsea Old Church, All Saints   6 E4
Chelsea Embankment SW3. 071-352 5627. Henry VIII and Jane Seymour married here in 1536. Original church dates from 1157, but the south chapel was rebuilt by Sir Thomas More. Severely bombed in 1941 and restored by Walter Godfrey. Many historic monuments.

London Central Mosque   1 A4
Hanover Gate, Regent's Park NW1. 071-724 3363. Graceful building completed 1978, the religious centre for London's Muslims. A 75ft (25m) high golden dome and rich interior – marble floors, Turkish tiles, Iranian carpets and Jordanian chandeliers.

St Bartholomew-the-Great   5 C1
West Smithfield EC1. 071-606 1575. Oldest church in London – the only surviving part of an Augustinian priory founded in 1123. Unusual oriel window and the only pre-Reformation font in the City. Many fine monuments.

St Clement Danes   4 F3
Strand WC2. 071-242 8282. First built by Danes in 9thC, rebuilt by Wren 1681. Destroyed during the Blitz, restored and rededicated in 1958 as the central church of the RAF. Bells ring 'Oranges and Lemons', made famous by the nursery rhyme of the same name.

St Giles Cripplegate   5 D1
Fore St EC2. 071-606 3630. 12thC church rebuilt 1537 and restored by Godfrey Allen 1952 after bombing. Milton is buried here. Remains of the London Wall in churchyard.

St James Piccadilly   4 D3
Piccadilly W1. 071-734 4511. Wren 1684. Restored by Sir Albert Richardson 1954 after serious bomb damage. Reredos, organ casing and font by Grinling Gibbons. Famous 'Father Smith' organ presented by Queen Mary 1691 and brought from Whitehall Palace.

St John Smith Square   4 F6
Smith Sq SW1. 071-222 2168. Nicknamed 'Queen Anne's Footstool'. Built 1721-8 by Archer, gutted by fire 1742. Interior redesigned, then blitzed 1941. Restored to original design by a charitable trust. Opened as a concert hall 1969.

St Margaret Westminster   4 F5
Parliament Sq SW1. 071-222 6382. Rebuilt 1486-1523 and after World War II. Splendid early 16thC east window and stained glass by Piper. Parish church of House of Commons since 1614. Samuel Pepys married here 1655, John Milton in 1656 and Winston Churchill in 1908. Caxton, Walter Raleigh and Admiral Blake are buried here.

St Martin-in-the-Fields   4 F4
Trafalgar Sq WC2. 071-930 1862. Founded 12thC, rebuilt many times. Present construction by Gibbs 1722-4 with famous spire and portico. In 1924 the first broadcast service was conducted from here. Charles II christened here 1630; Nell Gwynne, Hogarth, Sir Joshua Reynolds buried here. Brass rubbing centre, craft market, restaurant and gallery.

St Mary-le-Bow   5 D2
Cheapside EC2. 071-248 5139. Famous for its bells, used before World War II as time signal by BBC. True Cockneys are born within hearing distance of them. Rebuilt Wren 1670-83 and again by King 1956-62. Superb steeple – 217ft (66m).

St Paul's Cathedral   5 D2
Ludgate Hill EC4. 071-248 4619/2705. Wren's masterpiece is the fifth cathedral on this site. The Whispering Gallery in the dome is particularly impressive – so named because the quietest whisper carries from one side to the other – 107ft (33m) away. Choir stalls and organ by Grinling Gibbons. Nelson and the Duke of Wellington are buried here; the Prince and Princess of Wales were married here in 1981. *Open 07.15-18.00 Mon-Sun except during special services.* Free. Crypt *open 09.00-16.15 Mon-Sat;* Galleries *open 09.45-16.15 Mon-Sat.* Charge.

St Peter-upon-Cornhill   5 E2
Cornhill EC3. 071-626 9483. Very fine church by Wren, 1677-

87. Oldest church site in the City, reputedly AD179. Organ built by Schmidt. Fine carved screen.

Southwark Cathedral   **5 E4**

Borough High St SE1. 071-407 2939. Originally founded in the 7thC, this is one of London's earliest Gothic churches. The tower dates to 1520 and the collection of monuments includes an oak effigy of a knight, dating to around 1275. The Chapter House has been redeveloped and now includes a restaurant. Cathedral *open 08.30-18.00 Mon-Sun (from 07.30 Tue).* Chapter House Restaurant *open 10.00-16.00 Mon-Fri.*

Temple Church   **5 B2**

Inner Temple, Crown Office Row EC4. 071-797 8250. One of only four remaining early Gothic round churches built by the Knight Templars, 12thC-13thC.

Westminster Abbey   **4 F6**

Broad Sanctuary SW1. 071-222 5152. Original church founded by Edward the Confessor 1065. Rebuilding commenced 1245 by Henry III and largely completed by 1506. Towers completed by Hawksmoor 1734. Since William I it has been the coronation church of every new monarch and houses the coronation chair. Many royal and historic figures buried here, along with the Unknown Warrior, whose tomb represents the dead of World War I. Poets' Corner is the resting place of Dryden, Browning, Sheridan and Tennyson. Sculpted angels in south transept and fine tiled floors. *Open 09.30-16.00 Mon-Fri; 09.30-14.00 & 15.45-17.00 Sat. Closed Sun, services only.* Museum *open 10.30-16.00 Mon-Sun.* Small charge.

Westminster RC Cathedral   **4 D6**

Ashley Place SW1. 071-834 7452. The headquarters of the Catholic Church in Britain. Completed 1903, with glorious marble mosaics. Widest nave in England with the early 15thC statue of Our Lady and Child. *Open 06.45-20.00 Mon-Sun.*

London's bridges

Albert Bridge   **6 E4**

Three-span bridge 1871 by Ordish. Unusual rigid chain suspension. Tradition has it that soldiers crossing must break step because their marching rhythm may weaken the structure! Particularly beautiful at night when illuminated.

Chelsea Bridge   **7 B4**

Original bridge built 1858 by Page. Human bones and Roman and British weapons tell of an immense battle fought here. Entirely replaced in 1934 by a suspension bridge.

Lambeth Bridge   **7 E2**

The site of the first bridge at Lambeth was originally the only place where a coach and horses could cross the river. In 1633

Archbishop Laud sank the coach with his belongings whilst moving into Lambeth Palace! First bridge built 1861, replaced 1929.

London Bridge   5 E4
Reigned supreme as the only bridge for 500 years. Originally wooden construction built by Romans, replaced in 12thC with stone one carrying houses, shops and the heads of traitors on spikes. Replaced many times – in 1971 the granite construction by Rennie (1832) was shipped off in its entirety to Lake Havasu City, Arizona. Present bridge 1973.

Queen Elizabeth II Bridge
London's newest bridge, opened October 1991. The first bridge downstream since Tower Bridge built 1894. Designed to ease the weight of traffic through Dartford Tunnel. Largest of its type in Europe – twin towers 450ft (130m) high. Toll charges will be incurred until around the year 2005.

Tower Bridge   5 G4
Jones and Wolfe-Barry 1894. Designed to echo the Tower of London. It opens to allow tall ships to pass – each section of the double-bascule drawbridge weighs over 1000 tonnes but can be raised in under two minutes. High walkways afford excellent views of London and the Thames. Museum displays illustrate the workings of the bridge and a new permanent exhibition, 'The Celebration Story', will mark Tower Bridge's centenary year (1994) by bringing to life the history, human endeavour and engineering achievement which created this famous landmark. *Museum will be closed during 1993 for building of the new exhibition; phone for details of re-opening.*

Waterloo Bridge   4 G3
Rennie 1811. Opened on the anniversary of the Battle of Waterloo. Present bridge by Sir Giles Gilbert Scott 1937-42.

Westminster Bridge   4 F5
The watermen of the Thames were paid £25,000 in compensation when the bridge was begun in 1738. A stern warning went out when it opened – no dogs and the death penalty for anyone found defacing its walls! Present structure graceful cast iron, 1854 by Page.

Statues and monuments

Achilles   4 B4
Park Lane W1. 20ft (6.5m) bronze by Westmacott 1822. Caused an uproar as it was a nude statue dedicated by the 'women of England' to the Duke of Wellington.

Alfred the Great   5 D6
Trinity Church Sq SE1. Unknown origins, but undoubtedly the oldest statue in London, dating to the 14thC.

Boadicea   4 F5
Westminster Bridge SW1. Thornycroft, unveiled 1902. It

shows the famous British queen riding with her daughters in a chariot.

Charles I
4 F4

Trafalgar Sq SW1. Hubert le Sueur, 1675. Ordered to be destroyed in 1649, buried and kept safe until the Restoration in 1660. Royal Stuart Society lays a wreath here on the anniversary of his death, 30 January.

Sir Charles Chaplin
4 E3

Leicester Sq WC2. Doubleday, unveiled 1981 by the actor Sir Ralph Richardson. With his customary bowler hat and walking stick, he is appropriately surrounded by cinemas.

Sir Winston Churchill
4 F5

Parliament Sq SW1. 1973 by Ivor Roberts-Jones. Magnificent bronze statue of one of Britain's greatest statesmen, in naval overcoat, half-facing the House of Commons.

Oliver Cromwell
4 F6

Old Palace Yard SW1. Bronze by Thornycroft 1899. Holds a Bible in one hand and sword in the other. Paid for by Prime Minister Lord Rosebery as Parliament refused. Significantly, he stands with his back to the Houses of Parliament!

Elizabeth I
5 B2

St Dunstan-in-the-West, Fleet St EC4. Cast during the Queen's lifetime, 1586, by Kerwin. Originally stood over Lud Gate.

Eros
4 E3

Piccadilly Circus W1. Gilbert 1893. London's first aluminium statue, officially representing the Angel of Christian Charity. Paid for by public donations and restored in 1984.

Sir Thomas More
5 B2

Carey St WC2. Stone figure by Smith 1866. More was 'the faithful servant both of God and the King. Martyred 5 July 1535'.

Peter Pan
3 E4

Kensington Gardens W2. Frampton 1912. Delightful figure of the fictional fairy character. Erected overnight as a surprise for the children. Carved animals at the base have been worn away by the strokes of tiny hands.

Captain Scott
4 E4

Waterloo Place SW1. Bronze by Lady Scott, erected 1915, of her husband in full arctic kit.

Victoria Memorial
4 D5

In front of Buckingham Palace SW1. By Brock, 1911. Impressive memorial to Queen Victoria which includes a fine, dignified figure of the Queen, the best of many statues of her.

Duke of Wellington
4 B5

Hyde Park Corner SW1. Huge bronze figure by J.E. Boehm (1888) of the Duke astride his favourite horse, Copenhagen. He looks towards Apsley House (now the Wellington Museum) where he lived.

Commemorative plaques

Since 1866, blue plaques have been used to mark houses and other buildings associated with famous people or events. There are now nearly 400 of them commemorating the lives of architects, artists, composers, politicians, scientists, soldiers and writers. The following are a selection:

Baden-Powell, Robert Stephenson   **3 D5**
Founder of the Boy Scouts movement. Lived at 9 Hyde Park Gate SW7.

Berlioz, Hector   **4 C1**
Composer. Stayed at 58 Queen Anne St W1.

Bligh, William   **4 C2**
Captain of *HMS Bounty*. Lived at 17 South Molton St W1.

Browning, Elizabeth Barrett   **4 A1**
Poet and wife of poet Robert Browning. Lived at 99 Gloucester Place W1.

Brunel, Isambard Kingdom   **6 D5**
Civil engineer. Lived at 98 Cheyne Walk SW3.

Engels, Friedrich   **1 B2**
Political philosopher and novelist. Lived at 121 Regent's Park Rd NW1.

Gwynne, Nell   **4 E4**
Actress, mistress of Charles II. Lived at 79 Pall Mall SW1.

Handel, George Frideric   **4 C3**
Composer and musician. Lived and died at 25 Brook St W1.

Kipling, Rudyard   **4 F4**
Poet and story writer. Lived at 43 Villiers St WC2.

Marconi, Guglielmo Marchese   **3 B2**
Inventor and pioneer of wireless communication. Lived at 71 Hereford Rd W2.

Mozart, Wolfgang Amadeus   **7 A2**
Composer and musician. Composed his first symphony at 180 Ebury St SW1.

Pepys, Samuel   **5 C2**
Diarist. Born in a house on the site of Salisbury Court EC4.

Shaw, George Bernard   **2 E5**
Dramatist and essayist. Lived at 29 Fitzroy Sq W1.

Scott, Captain Robert Falcon   **6 E4**
Antarctic explorer. Lived at 56 Oakley St SW3, from where he left on his last fatal journey.

Turner, Joseph Mallord William   **6 D5**
Painter. Lived at 119 Cheyne Walk SW3.

Wilde, Oscar Fingall O'Flahertie   **6 F4**
Poet, dramatist and wit. Lived at 34 Tite St SW3.

Wren, Sir Christopher   **5 D3**
Architect. Lived at 49 Bankside SE1.

ANNUAL EVENTS

London plays host to a vast number of annual events, from colourful ceremonies to more obscure London customs such as the Doggett's Coat & Badge Race. For exact dates, times and places, where not given, contact one of the London Tourist Board information centres (see page 20).

Daily ceremonies

Contact the London Tourist Board Information Centre, Victoria Station Forecourt SW1 (071-730 3488) for further information.

Ceremony of the Keys   **5 G3**
HM Tower of London, Tower Hill EC3. 071-709 0765. The Chief Warder of the Yeomen Warders, with an escort from the Brigade of Guards, locks the West Gates, the Middle Tower and Byward Tower. Listen out for the words spoken every night for 700 years – 'Halt! Who comes there?' 'The keys.' 'Whose keys?' 'Queen Elizabeth II's keys.' 'Pass the keys. All's well.' *21.40 Mon-Sun by written application, well in advance and enclosing a stamped addressed envelope, to the Governor, Queen's House, HM Tower of London EC3. Free.*

Changing the Guard   **4 D5**
Buckingham Palace SW1. Takes place inside the palace railings (in *summer* the crowds make it difficult to see much). The custom began in the days when the Life Guards were responsible for protecting the life of the monarch. An alternative is to see the Guards on their way from Chelsea or Wellington Barracks. They leave Chelsea at *10.45* and Wellington at *11.00*. The palace ceremony takes place at *11.30 every day in summer, alternate days in winter.*
Also at **St James's Palace (4 D4)** at *11.15;* **Whitehall (4 F4)** at *11.00 Mon-Sat, 10.00 Sun,* leaving Hyde Park Barracks *10.38 Mon-Sat, 09.39 Sun;* and **Windsor Castle**, Windsor, Berks (0753) 868286 at *11.00-11.30 every day in summer, alternate days in winter. Free.*

Other daily events

Speakers' Corner   **4 A3**
Marble Arch corner of Hyde Park. A remaining vestige of the British tradition of free speech is this institution of impromptu

discourses by unknown orators, usually on religion or politics. Most lively on *Sun*. Also at Lincoln's Inn Fields (**5 A2**) and Tower Hill (**5 G3**) *Mon-Fri lunchtime*. Free.

Feeding the pigeons   **4 F4**

Trafalgar Sq WC2. A famous tradition. You will soon find yourself accosted by touts who want to sell you bird-seed and photographs of yourself. Beware, if you buy any seed, the pigeons are likely to land on your head!

Annual events

JANUARY
International Boat Show   **6 A3**

Earl's Court Exhibition Centre, Warwick Rd SW5. 071-385 1200. The latest pleasure crafts, yachts and equipment to marvel at. Largest boat show in Europe. *Early Jan*. Charge.

January sales

Most stores have stock-clearing sales after the Christmas shopping spree. Some fantastic bargains to be had, especially at Harrods, but these go quickly and there are always huge crowds, so get there early. The real fanatics camp outside the stores, sometimes for days beforehand in a bid to be first in.

Lord Mayor of Westminster's New Year's Day   **4 D4**
Parade

Information: 081-992 9600. One of the largest parades in Europe, with some 5000 performers. Marching bands, colourful floats and veteran vehicles. Starts at Piccadilly and ends at Hyde Park (**4 B4**) where the entertainment continues. *1 Jan*. Free.

Royal Epiphany Gifts   **4 D4**

Chapel Royal, St James's Place, Marlborough Rd SW1. Picturesque ceremony involving two 'Gentlemen Ushers' offering gold, frankincense and myrrh on behalf of the Queen. *Admission by ticket only; apply to the above address. 11.30, 6 Jan*. Free.

FEBRUARY
Chinese New Year Festival   **4 E3**

Chinatown, Gerrard St W1. Noisy, colourful affair in the heart of the West End to celebrate Chinese New Year. Papier-mâché dragons, extravagant costumes and brightly-lit festivities animate the whole area. *Jan or Feb*. Free.

Soho Pancake Day Race   **4 D3**

Carnaby St W1. Information: 071-287 0907. Pancakes are the traditional food eaten on Shrove Tuesday, the day before the beginning of Lent. Watch various teams running with frying pans and tossing their pancakes as they go. *End Feb or during Mar, depending on when Easter falls*. Free.

Mar, depending on when Easter falls. Free.
MARCH
Chelsea Antiques Fair   6 E3
Chelsea Old Town Hall, King's Rd SW3. 071-352 3619. Good selection of antiques and antiquities, with some real bargains. *Mid Mar.*
John Stow Memorial Service   5 F2
Church of St Andrew Undershaft, St Mary Axe EC3. The Lord Mayor attends this commemoration of London's first historian and places a new quill pen in the hand of Stow's statue. *11.30 Sun in Mar or Apr.* Free.
Oxford v Cambridge Boat Race
River Thames, Putney SW15 to Mortlake SW14. The annual rowing challenge between the dark and light blues (Oxford and Cambridge universities) has taken place since 1845. Plenty of vantage points from bridges, banks or riverside pubs – advisable to get there early for a good view. *Sat afternoon in Mar or Apr.* Free.

APRIL
Easter Show   6 F5
Battersea Park SW11. Colourful carnival; jugglers, stilt walkers and bands. Plus fairground, side stalls and various stage acts. *Easter Sun.*
London Harness Horse Parade   1 C4
Regent's Park NW1. Fine breeds from Shires and Somersets to lighter-weight horses and ponies, carts, brewer's vans and drays are paraded around the Inner Circle at *12.00.* Judging starts at *09.30* and the public can inspect the horses before the parade. *Easter Mon.* Free.
London Marathon
Information: 081-948 7935. The world's largest road race with competitors a mixture of international marathon runners, serious runners, joggers, celebrities and fancy dress 'fun' runners (usually raising money for charity). Good atmosphere with large crowds at both the start (Greenwich Park SE10) and finish (Westminster Bridge SW1 – **4 F5**). *Late Apr.* Free to spectators.
Tower of London Church Parade   5 G3
Tower of London, Tower Hill EC3. 071-709 0765. The Yeomen Warders, in state dress, are inspected and parade before and after morning service at *11.00 Easter Sun.* Free.

MAY
Chelsea Flower Show   7 A3
Chelsea Royal Hospital, Royal Hospital Rd SW3. 071-834 4333. Recorded information: 071-828 1744. Superb floral displays burst into bloom in the grounds of the Royal Hospital.

vegetable displays, garden equipment and other green-fingered accessories. *For four days, third week of May.* Charge.

FA Cup Final
Wembley Stadium, Wembley, Middx. 081-900 1234. Climax of the English football season. *Some tickets from the above number, but the majority go to the two clubs whose teams are participating. Early May.* Charge.

Glyndebourne Festival Opera Season
Glyndebourne, nr Lewes, E. Sussex. (0273) 541111. Well-heeled Londoners don evening dress to hear superlative singing and dine out on the lawn, if the summer weather permits! Performances *May-Aug.* Charge.

Open Air Art Exhibitions
Artists display their work for the public to view (and hopefully buy!).
Victoria Embankment Gardens WC2 (**4 F4**) – *2-14 May & Mon-Sat during Aug.*
Royal Ave, King's Rd SW3 (**6 F3**) – *May-Oct 11.00-18.00 Sat.*
Works are also displayed against the railings on the Green Park side of Piccadilly (**4 C4**) and along Bayswater Road outside Kensington Gardens and Hyde Park (**3 D3**). *Sun morning all year round.* Free.

Rugby League Challenge Cup Final
Wembley Stadium, Wembley, Middx. Climax of the English Rugby League season, battled out in the mud at Wembley. *Contact the Rugby Football League (0532) 623637 for details. Late Apr/early May.* Charge.

Rugby Union Cup Final
Twickenham Rugby Football Ground, Whitton Rd, Twickenham, Middx. *Phone 081-892 8161 for details. Early May.* Charge.

JUNE
Beating the Retreat   4 F4
Horse Guards' Parade SW1. 071-839 6815. Colourful military display of marching and drilling bands acknowledging the 'retreat' or setting of the sun. Evening floodlit performances especially delightful. *For tickets phone 071-930 0292. Early Jun.* Charge.

Derby Day
Epsom Racecourse, Epsom, Surrey. (0373) 726311. World-famous flat horserace. Also a fun fair and side shows. *1st week in Jun.* Charge.

Election of the Sheriffs of the City of London   5 D2
Guildhall EC2. 071-606 3030. Lord Mayor and Aldermen of the City of London take part in a colourful ceremony. Tradition

dictates that posies are carried to ward off 'the plague'. *Midsummer's Day, unless it falls on a Sat or Sun.* Free.

Founder's Day 7 A3
Chelsea Royal Hospital, Royal Hospital Rd SW3. 071-730 0161. Chelsea pensioners parade in their colourful uniforms for inspection, sometimes by royalty. *Early Jun.* Free.

The Garter Ceremony
St George's Chapel, Windsor, Berks. Service dating from 14thC attended by the Queen. Preceded by procession with the Household Cavalry and Yeomen of the Guard. *Mon afternoon of Ascot week (usually 3rd week in Jun).* Free.

Kenwood Lakeside Concerts
Kenwood House, Hampstead Lane NW3. 071-973 3427. Bookings: 071-379 4444. Classical concerts beside Kenwood Lake on Hampstead Heath performed by some of the most famous orchestras in the world. Often end with spectacular firework displays. *Sat evenings Jun-Aug.* Charge.

Lord's Test Match
Lord's Cricket Ground, St John's Wood Rd NW8. 071-289 1611/5. Recorded information on state of play: 071-289 8011. Although confusing for the beginner, cricket is a British institution. The Test Match takes place here over *three or five days Jun or Jul.* Charge.

Royal Academy Summer Art Exhibition 4 D3
Royal Academy, Burlington House, Piccadilly W1. 071-439 7438. Aspiring Cézannes and Hockneys enter their works to be admired and hopefully bought! Huge mixture of styles from amateur-looking oils to beautifully-crafted architectural designs. Be prepared for long queues. *Jun-mid Aug.* Charge.

Royal Ascot Races
Ascot Racecourse, Ascot, Berks. (0344) 22211. Famous event where hats and horses vie for attention. The Queen and other members of the royal party travel the course in open carriages each day before the race. *Three days – usually 3rd week in Jun.* Charge.

Trooping the Colour
Colourful pageant and procession to celebrate the Queen's official birthday. Royal party leaves Buckingham Palace (**4 D5**) at around *10.30* and proceeds along the Mall (**4 D5**) to Horse Guards' Parade (**4 F4**), then to Whitehall (**4 F4**) and back again. *Tickets awarded by ballot from The Brigade Major, Trooping the Colour, Household Division, Horse Guards' Parade SW1 (enclose a stamped addressed envelope). 11.00 Sat nearest 11 Jun.* Charge.

Wimbledon Lawn Tennis Championships
Church Rd SW19. Recorded information: 081-946 2244. Height of the tennis circuit tournaments and one of the most famous championships in the world. Early evening is the best

time to go to avoid the crowds. *Tickets for Centre Court, No.1 and No.2 Court are awarded by public ballot, but you can queue for tickets for the other courts on the day of play. 14.00 Mon-Sat. Last week Jun & first week Jul.* Charge.

JULY
City of London Festival
Information: 071-377 0540/248 4260. Arts festival held in the Barbican (**5 D1**), the Tower of London (**5 G3**), Mansion House (**5 E2**), St Paul's Cathedral (**5 D2**), many fine churches and the City's open spaces. Concerts, opera, exhibitions, poetry, drama, dance, jazz and many varied street events. *Three weeks in Jul.* Some events free, some charge.
Doggett's Coat & Badge Race
Information: 071-626 3531. London Bridge (**5 E4**) to Chelsea Bridge (**7 B4**). Started 1715 to commemorate the accession of King George I. Sometimes called the 'Watermen's Derby', after the men who used to rule London's transport on the Thames, it is limited to six recently-qualified watermen. Colourful and fun event. *Late Jul.* Free.
Henley Royal Regatta
Henley-on-Thames, Oxon. (0491) 572153. Steeped in tradition, where smart outfits and even smarter picnics try to outdo each other on the riverbank whilst watching the skilled rowers do their stuff. *For exact dates phone the above number. Early Jul.* Free in public areas.
Proms (Henry Wood Promenade Concerts)   3 E5
Royal Albert Hall, Kensington Gore SW7. 071-589 8212. Classical music festival culminating in the famous Last Night of the Proms at the Royal Albert Hall (see page 51). *Late Jul until Sep.* Charge.
Royal Tournament   6 A3
Earl's Court Exhibition Centre, Warwick Rd SW5. 071-373 8141. Impressive military spectacle presented by the armed forces with much pageantry, military bands and daring feats. *Two weeks mid Jul.* Charge.
Swan Upping
Information: 071-236 1863. London Bridge (**5 E4**) to Henley, Berks. Ownership of the swans on the Thames is divided between the Dyers' Company, the Vintners' Company and the Sovereign. The Queen's Swan Keeper leads the keepers of the other companies and the swanherds to a fleet of boats, banners flying, for the trip up the reaches from London as far as Henley for the swan census. The cygnets are branded by nicking their beaks – one nick for the Dyers'; two for the Vintners'; the Sovereign's are left unmarked. *Phone in advance to find out exactly where the fleet is at any one time. Jul-Aug.* Free.

AUGUST
Notting Hill Carnival 3 A3

Ladbroke Grove and Notting Hill W11. Started originally as a celebration of West Indian culture, a lively, noisy, colourful event with music, dancing in the streets and processions. *Sun* is children's day, and the main processions take place on *Bank hol Mon. Last Mon in Aug.* Free.

SEPTEMBER
Election of Lord Mayor of London 5 D2

St Lawrence Jewry, Gresham St EC2 to the Guildhall EC2. 071-606 3030. Colourful procession to celebrate the election of the new Lord Mayor of London. *Michaelmas Day.* Free.

Last Night of the Proms 3 E5

Royal Albert Hall, Kensington Gore SW7. 071-589 8212. The culmination of the Proms concerts. Traditional rousing performance of *Land of Hope and Glory. Tickets by qualification system only – contact the above address. Mid Sep.* Charge.

OCTOBER
Her Majesty's Judges & Queen's Counsels 4 F6
Annual Breakfast

After a special service at Westminster Abbey, there is a procession to the House of Lords for the opening of the Law Term. *1 Oct.* Free.

Horse of the Year Show

Wembley Arena, Wembley, Middx. 081-902 8833. Fine showjumping with many of the world-famous competitors under one roof. *Early Oct.* Charge.

NOVEMBER
Admission of the Lord Mayor Elect 5 D2

Guildhall EC2. 071-606 3030. The Lord Mayor takes office. Colourful ceremony including the handing over of insignia by the former Lord Mayor. *Fri before Lord Mayor's Show. Mid Nov.* Free.

Christmas lights 4 D2

Oxford St and Regent St W1. Bright and imaginative illuminations line the streets and shop windows to celebrate the season. Ceremoniously switched on in *early Nov.* Free.

Guy Fawkes Night

Bonfires are lit all over London and Britain to commemorate the discovery of the Gunpowder Plot of 1605, by which Guy Fawkes and his fellow conspirators intended to blow up James I and Parliament. Organised public events are the safest and usually the most spectacular. *Evening 5 Nov.* Charge for organised displays.

London to Brighton Veteran Car Run 3 G4

Serpentine Rd, Hyde Park W2. Information: 081-686 2525.

First held on 'Emancipation Day' in 1896 which celebrated the abolition of the Act stipulating that a car must be preceded by a person walking with a red flag at 2 miles per hour. A colourful event with the contestants in period costume; only open to cars made before 1905. They start at *08.00* and aim to reach Brighton by *16.00. First Sun in Nov.* Free.

Lord Mayor's Procession & Show
The newly-elected Lord Mayor is driven in the 1756 State Coach, with a procession of about 140 floats, from the Guildhall (**5 D2**) to the Law Courts (**5 B2**) to be received and sworn in by the Lord Chief Justice. Biggest ceremonial event in the City. *11.10 second Sat in Nov.* Free.

Remembrance Sunday   4 F5
The Cenotaph, Whitehall SW1. Service attended by the Queen and the Prime Minister to honour the dead of both World Wars. Takes place at the eleventh hour of the eleventh day (or nearest Sun) of the eleventh month – the anniversary of the armistice of World War I. Poppies sold in the street to raise money for ex-servicemen. Get there early for a good view. *11.00 Sun nearest 11 Nov.* Free.

State Opening of Parliament
The Queen, in the Irish State Coach, is driven from Buckingham Palace (**4 D5**) to the House of Lords (**4 F5**) to open Parliament after the summer recess. Good views from the north side of The Mall – get there early. *10.30 1st week Nov.* Free.

DECEMBER
Carol services   4 F6
Westminster Abbey, Broad Sanctuary SW1. 071-222 7110. Carol services on *26, 27 & 28 Dec.* Free.

Carol singing   4 F4
Trafalgar Sq WC2. Carols are recorded on tape so you can just listen or sing along! *All through Dec.* Free.

Christmas Tree   4 F4
Trafalgar Sq WC2. Each year the citizens of Oslo donate a Norwegian spruce (a custom dating from World War II). It is brightly lit from *16.00* and carols are sung around it. *Mid Dec-6 Jan (Twelfth Night).* Free.

New Year's Eve   4 F4
Trafalgar Sq WC2. Thousands gather in the square to bring in the New Year with massed singing of *Auld Lang Syne* and dancing round the fountains. Listen out for Big Ben tolling midnight. *31 Dec.* Free.

Tower of London Church Parade   5 G3
Tower of London, Tower Hill EC3. 071-709 0765. The Yeomen Warders, in state dress, are inspected and parade before and after morning service. *11.00 Sun before Xmas.* Free.

MUSEUMS & GALLERIES

London's national museums and galleries contain some of the richest treasures in the world collected during British explorations. They range from the vast British Museum to more recent and specialist additions and many now incorporate interactive displays and exhibits. Apart from the national art collections in the Tate Gallery, the National Gallery and the National Portrait Gallery, London is further enriched by other, once private, collections, now open to the public. It has long been a tradition that national museums and galleries are free, *but some have now found it necessary to introduce either* voluntary contributions *or a* fixed admission fee. *Special exhibitions usually incur an* entrance fee.

Bank of England Museum   **5 E2**
Bank of England, Bartholomew Lane EC2. 071-601 5545. Charts the Bank's history from 1694 to the high-tech world of modern banking. Houses unique English banknotes, gold bars and the Bank's silver collection. *Open Easter-Sep 10.00-17.00 Mon-Fri, 11.00-17.00 Sat, Sun & Bank hols; Oct-Easter 10.00-17.00 Mon-Fri only.* Free.

HMS Belfast   **5 F4**
Symons Wharf, Vine Lane SE1. 071-407 6434. Cruiser built for the Royal Navy; now a museum showing its role during wartime. Film shows and lectures. *Open Oct-Mar 10.00-16.00 Mon-Sun; Apr-Sep 10.00-18.00 Mon-Sun.* Charge.

British Museum   **1 G6**
Great Russell St WC1. 071-636 1555. The world's greatest collection of antiquities and the national collection of archaeology and ethnography with four million (or so!) objects ranging from pre-historic to modern. Pick up a copy of the free information map at the entrance to help you plan your way around. Highlights include the Rosetta Stone; Roman pavements; the Elgin marbles; 'Pete Marsh', the 2000-year-old murdered Lindow man found preserved in a Cheshire bog; and the Sutton Hoo treasures from the burial site of a 7thC Anglo-Saxon king. Also famous for mummies including those of humans, cats, crocodiles and even baboons. Domed Reading Room (1857) where Karl Marx studied and wrote *Das Kapital*

(open to members only). Next to the main hall is the **British Library** which contains, by law, one copy of every book, periodical or newspaper printed in Great Britain. Collection includes two of the four Magna Cartas, the Lindisfarne Gospels and Shakespeare's first folio. Restaurant. Café. Excellent shop. *Guided tours (1½ hrs) at 10.30, 11.00, 13.30 & 14.00 Mon-Sat, 14.45, 15.15 & 15.45 Sun.* Museum *open 10.00-17.00 Mon-Sat, 14.30-18.00 Sun.* Free (charge for special exhibitions and guided tours).

Cabinet War Rooms   **4 F5**
Clive Steps, King Charles St SW1. 071-930 6961. Intriguing underground suite of 19 rooms used by Winston Churchill and his War Cabinet from August 1939-September 1945 as a meeting, planning and information centre. See Winston's bedroom and the desk from which he made some of his famous war-time broadcasts. *Personal sound guide included in entrance fee. Open 10.00-17.15 Mon-Sun.* Charge.

Commonwealth Institute   **3 B6**
230 Kensington High St W8. 071-603 4535. Near the grand gates of Holland Park, founded in 1887 to promote knowledge of Queen Victoria's Empire. Fun, friendly and lively, with lots of interactive and often humorous displays to show the history, people, landscapes, wildlife and crafts of the Commonwealth. Restaurant. Shop. *Open 10.00-17.00 Mon-Sat, 14.00-17.00 Sun.* Free (charge for special exhibitions).

Courtauld Institute Galleries   **4 G3**
Somerset House, Strand WC2. 071-873 2526. Notable assembly of paintings, furniture and drawings from six private collections. Fine examples of baroque furniture, Flemish and Italian Old Masters, the Mark Gambier-Parry Bequest and works by Manet, Renoir, Cézanne, van Gogh and Gauguin. *Open 10.00-18.00 Mon-Sat, 14.00-18.00 Sun.* Charge.

Design Museum   **5 G4**
Butler's Wharf, Shad Thames SE1. 071-407 6261. Founded by Sir Terence Conran, shows examples of design past, present and future through a number of provocative exhibits. Furniture, gadgets and graphics. Blueprint Café renowned for good food. Bookshop, library. *Tours by prior arrangement. Open 10.30-17.30 Mon-Sun.* Charge.

Dulwich Picture Gallery
College Rd, Dulwich SE21. 081-693 5254. The first public art gallery in England (1814). Works by Claude, Cuyp, Rembrandt (including his portrait of Jacob II de Gheyn – stolen four times), Rubens, van Dyck, Gainsborough, Hogarth, Canaletto and Watteau. Shop. *Guided tour 15.00 Sat & Sun (included in entrance fee). Open 10.00-13.00 & 14.00-17.00 Tue-Fri, 10.00-17.00 Sat, 14.00-17.00 Sun. Closed Mon.* Charge.

Geffrye Museum
Kingsland Rd, Hackney E2. 071-739 9893. Housed in several early 18thC almshouses, exhibitions of the British living room from Tudor times to the 1950s including the pre-fabs of the 1940s, a panelled Elizabethan Room, an early Georgian Room and two stylish 1930s rooms. Café. Shop. Gardens. *Open 10.00-17.00 Tue-Sat, 14.00-17.00 Sun.* Free.

Hayward Gallery 5 A4
South Bank Centre SE1. 071-928 3144. Main venue for large-scale temporary exhibitions of both historical and contemporary art from America, Europe and Britain. Shop. *Open 10.00-18.00 Mon-Sun (to 20.00 Tue & Wed). Closed between exhibitions.* Charge (reduced admission price *Mon*).

Imperial War Museum 5 B6
Lambeth Rd SE1. 071-416 5000. Popular museum concentrating on both the human and mechanical aspects of war. Vast collection of tanks, weapons and aircraft including a Mark I Spitfire. The Blitz Experience lets you see, feel and hear what it was like to be in London during the bombing of the 1940s. Operation Jericho is a flight simulator allowing you to experience flying with the RAF to release captured Resistance fighters. Good café. Shop. *Open 10.00-18.00 Mon-Sun.* Charge.

Institute of Contemporary Arts (ICA) 4 E4
The Mall SW1. 071-930 3647. Three galleries with changing contemporary art exhibitions. Widely regarded as one of the most innovative art venues in the country. Also two cinemas, a theatre and video library. Restaurant. Café/bar. Bookshop. *Open 12.00-23.00* (galleries *to 19.30) Mon-Sun.*

Jewish Museum 1 F5
Woburn House, Tavistock Sq WC1. 071-388 4525. Anglo-Jewish life, its history and traditions illustrated by ceremonial and ritual objects. *Open 10.00-16.00 Tue, Wed & Thur, 10.00-13.00 Fri & Sun (last admission 30 mins before closing time). Closed Mon, Sat & Jewish hols.* Donation requested.

London Planetarium 1 C5
Marylebone Rd NW1. 071-486 1121. Mind-boggling journey amongst the stars, space and cosmos! Thousands of projected images become clear with an expert guide to explain the astronomical mysteries. Shows *every 40 mins Mon-Sun.* First show *10.20;* last show *17.00.* Charge (combined entrance ticket with Madame Tussaud's available).

London Toy & Model Museum 3 D3
21 Craven Hill W2. 071-262 9450. Vast collection of dolls, model cars, tin soldiers and countless other toys, spanning over 100 years. Also model railway and carousel ride. Café. *Open 10.00-17.30 Mon-Sat, 11.00-17.30 Sun.* Charge.

London Transport Museum   4 G3
39 Wellington St WC2. 071-379 6344. Story of London's
passenger transport system told through moving and static
exhibits. 'Drive' modern-day tubes and buses and work the
points and signals in a tunnel. New gallery housing London
Transport's poster collection. Shop. *Open 10.00-18.00 (last
admission 17.15) Mon-Sun.* Charge. *The museum will be
closed during 1993 for major refurbishment. Phone for details.*

Madame Tussaud's   1 C5
Marylebone Rd NW1. 071-935 6861. Amongst the waxwork
effigies of the famous and notorious meet the Royal Family,
Pavarotti, Nelson Mandela and Cher. Murderers lurk in the
Chamber of Horrors. Celebrities mingle at 'The Garden Party'.
Enjoy the sights and sounds of the seaside at 'The Promenade
Pier Café'. Experience some of the greatest events that have
shaped London's heritage at 'The Spirit of London', Madame
Tussaud's newest exhibition where visitors journey through
400 years of London's history in a replica of a black taxi cab.
Open 10.00-17.30 Mon-Fri, 09.30-17.30 Sat & Sun. Charge.

Museum of London   2 E6
London Wall EC2. 071-600 3699. London's biography from
pre-history to present day with a variety of costumes and
archaeological finds. Reconstructions include a Roman
kitchen, the devastation of the Great Fire in 1666, a ghoulish
cell from Newgate Prison, and Selfridges' 1920s art deco lifts.
Restaurant. Shop. *Open 10.00-18.00 Tue-Sat, 12.00-18.00
Sun. Closed Mon except Bank hols.* Charge.

Museum of Mankind   4 D3
6 Burlington Gdns W1. 071-437 2224. Ethnographic
Department of the British Museum. Contains the world's
largest and best collection of artefacts, clothing and housing
from areas in the Americas, Oceania and Africa. *Open 10.00-
17.00 Mon-Sat, 14.30-18.00 Sun.* Free.

Museum of the Moving Image (MOMI)   5 B4
South Bank SE1. 071-928 3535. The story of moving images
from Chinese shadow theatre to film, television and satellite.
Actors and presenters help you to read the news or animate a
cartoon. Frequently changing displays and plenty of moving
exhibits. Restaurant. Bar. Shop. *Open 10.00-18.00 (last admission 17.00) Mon-Sun.* Charge.

National Gallery   4 F3
Trafalgar Sq WC2. 071-839 3321. The nation's major collection
of historical paintings, founded in 1824, covering European
schools from the 13thC-20thC. A leaflet, available at the
entrance, leads you to the 16 most famous paintings. Daily
tours also highlight selected works. Famous painters include
Rembrandt, Rubens, Frans Hals, van Dyck, El Greco, Cézanne,

Monet and van Gogh. The Sainsbury Wing, opened in 1990, houses a collection of early Renaissance paintings including works by Botticelli, Raphael and Titian with great attention paid to the display of the paintings as well as the works themselves. Restaurant. Café/bar. Shop. *Regular guided tours every day (contact the information desk for times). Open 10.00-18.00 Mon-Sat, 14.00-18.00 Sun.* Free.

National Maritime Museum
Romney Rd, Greenwich SE10. 081-858 4422. In a beautiful riverside setting and incorporating the Old Royal Observatory and Queen's House, this is the world's largest collection of boats and navigational instruments. Ships' models, carved figureheads, weapons, pictures and fine silver collections tell the story of Britain and the sea, its navy, merchants and explorers. *Open Apr-Sep 10.00-18.00 Mon-Sat, 12.00-18.00 Sun; Oct-Mar 10.00-17.00 Mon-Sat, 14.00-17.00 Sun.* Charge.

National Portrait Gallery   4 F3
2 St Martin's Place WC2. 071-306 0055. The former stipulation that for inclusion in the National Portrait Gallery you had to be dead has now been relaxed! Start on the fifth floor and work your way down for a comprehensive, chronological look at portraits of the famous and infamous from Richard II and William Shakespeare to Mick Jagger and Beatrix Potter. Special exhibitions on famous people in the arts, sciences, politics and armed forces; also sculptures, miniatures, drawings and caricatures. Café. Bookshop. *Open 10.00-17.00 Mon-Fri, 10.00-18.00 Sat, 14.00-18.00 Sun.* Free.

National Postal Museum   5 D2
King Edward Bldg, King Edward St EC1. 071-239 5420. Thousands of stamps, stamp books and the Penny Black franked as the world's first stamp on May 6 1840. *Open 09.30-16.30 Mon-Fri.* Free.

Natural History Museum & Geological Museum   6 D1
Cromwell Rd SW7. 071-938 9123. The Natural History Museum incorporates the Geological Museum, and displays a full range of exhibitions featuring the earth itself, known as the Earth Galleries of the Natural History Museum. Advanced and innovative methods of display involve, interest and entertain visitors of all ages. Special effects include a simulated earthquake experience. Among the most impressive sights is the massive skeleton of one of the largest land animals, Diplodocus, as well as the life-size model of a 90ft (27.5m) blue whale. The New Dinosaur exhibition looks at every aspect of how dinosaurs lived and died, with large specimens and models. Restaurant. Café. Shop. Both *open 10.00-18.00 Mon-Sat, 11.00-18.00 Sun.* Charge (free *16.30-18.00 Mon-Fri, 17.00-18.00 Sun & Bank hols).*

Public Record Office 5 B2

Chancery Lane WC2. 081-876 3444. Public records from the Norman invasion to the latest census, along with treaties, writs and state papers. Star attraction is the *Domesday Book*, a detailed survey of England in 1086. To trace your roots go to St Catherine's House, 10 Kingsway WC2 (071-242 0262) where the register of births, marriages and deaths is kept. *Open 10.00-16.45 Mon-Fri.* Free.

Queen's Gallery 4 C5

Buckingham Palace, Buckingham Palace Rd SW1. 071-930 4832. The only part of Buckingham Palace open to the public, containing exhibits selected from the Royal art collection, regarded as one of the world's finest. Works by Rembrandt, Vermeer, Rubens, Holbein and Canaletto, as well as Sèvres porcelain, stamps and drawings. Shop. *Open Mar-Dec 10.00-17.00 Tue-Sat, 14.00-17.00 Sun. Last admission 16.30. Closed Mon except Bank hols.* Charge.

Royal Academy of Arts 4 D3

Burlington House, Piccadilly W1. 071-439 7438. Holds a series of important special-loan exhibitions throughout the year. Famous for its annual 'Summer Exhibition' which displays thousands of works by living artists for view and sale. Can get very crowded at weekends. Café. Good shop. *Open 10.00-18.00 Mon-Sun.* Charge.

Royal Air Force Museum

Grahame Park Way, Hendon NW9. 081-205 2266. The first national museum covering all aspects of the RAF and its predecessor, the RFC. There are 70 full-size aircraft displayed in hangars on a former wartime airfield. See the tiny Bleriot monoplane, Sopwith Camel, Spitfire, Vulcan, Wellington, Lancaster and others. The history of flight is told through equipment, paintings and documents and you can try your hand at piloting a low-flying Tornado in a simulator. The Battle of Britain Hall has British, German and Italian aircraft including Spitfires, Hurricanes and a Messerschmidt. Good restaurant. Shop. *Open 10.00-18.00 Mon-Sun.* Charge.

Science Museum 6 D1

Exhibition Rd SW7. 071-938 8000. One of the three great national museums covering science, technology and medicine. Includes many historic exhibits as well as more modern ones, like the command module of Apollo 10. Ranging from a tiny tea-making machine of 1904 to huge steam locomotives, the exhibits show how modern scientific and industrial man has emerged. Plenty of hands-on exhibits and interactive displays, especially in the Flight Lab near the Aeronautics Gallery (third floor), and in the Launch Pad (first floor). On the fourth and fifth floors is the Wellcome Museum of the History of

Medicine with exhibits covering human history from the neolithic age to the 1980s. *Open 10.00-18.00 Mon-Sat, 11.00-18.00 Sun*. Charge.

Shakespeare Globe Museum 5 D4

1 Bear Gdns, Bankside SE1. 071-928 6342. Exhibition of Shakespearian Theatre in a converted warehouse on the site of the last bear-bating ring to be used in London. A working reconstruction of Shakespeare's first Globe Theatre, following the original designs of 1599, is being constructed 300ft (91m) away. *Open 10.00-17.00 Mon-Sat, 14.00-17.30 Sun*. Charge.

Sherlock Holmes Museum 1 B5

221b Baker St NW1. 071-935 8866. Allegedly the house on which Conan Doyle modelled his imaginary 221b. The great detective's domestic world has been recreated based on detailed study of the stories. *Open 10.00-18.00 Mon-Sun*. Charge.

Sir John Soane's Museum 5 A2

13 Lincoln's Inn Fields WC1. 071-405 2107. Britain's smallest and most unusual national museum in the former home of Sir John Soane, one of England's most renowned and respected architects. Amongst the treasures are Hogarth's paintings the *Rake's Progress* and the *Election* series; antiquities, including the sarcophagus of Seti I (1370BC) found in the Valley of the Kings; and paintings by Turner, Watteau, Reynolds and Canaletto. *Guided tour 14.30 Sat. Open 10.00-17.00 Tue-Sat*. Charge.

Tate Gallery 7 E2

Millbank SW1. 071-821 1313. Named after sugar millionaire, Sir Henry Tate, who donated his Victorian paintings as its foundation. It is both the museum of British art, with a collection from the 16thC to around 1900, and holder of the national collection of international modern art. Works range from Impressionist to present day with often controversial new exhibits. The Clore Gallery holds the permanent Turner Bequest, including 300 paintings and 20,000 drawings by J.M.W. Turner. Due to the size of its collection, the Tate operates a policy of annual rotation, as they can only show a percentage of the works at any one time. Thus the star attractions mentioned below may or may not be on display when you visit – *phone the gallery in advance to avoid disappointment*. You may see Hogarth's self-portrait, Constable's *Flatford Mill*, William Blake's illustrations for Milton's *Paradise Lost*, or works by Monet, Seurat, Cézanne, Degas, Picasso, Matisse, Mondrian and British painters such as David Hockney, Ben Nicolson, and Augustus and Gwen John. Restaurant. Café. Excellent shop. *Regular guided tours Mon-Fri (contact the information desk for times). Open 10.00-17.50 Mon-Sat, 14.00-17.50 Sun*. Free (charge for special exhibitions).

Theatre Museum   4 F3
Russell St WC2. 071-836 7891. A branch of the Victoria &
Albert Museum, right in the heart of 'theatreland' and the
perfect place to discover the history of the English stage since
the 17thC. Magnificent collection of playbills, programmes,
prompt books, drawings, photos, models, costumes and
props. Café. Shop. *Open 11.00-19.00 Tue-Sun.* Charge.

Tower Hill Pageant   5 G3
Tower Hill Terrace EC3. 071-709 0081. London's first 'dark ride'
museum tells the story of 2000 years of the City of London.
Automated cars take you past life-like scenes depicting
London's waterfront from early Roman settlements to the Blitz.
Fascinating discoveries of recent archaeological waterfront
excavations, dating from Roman, Saxon and medieval times,
are also on display. Café. Shop. *Open Apr-Oct 09.30-17.30 Mon-
Sun; Nov-Mar 09.30-16.30 Mon-Sun.* Charge.

Tower of London   5 G3
Tower Hill EC3. 071-709 0765. Several museums and the
Crown Jewels in the Jewel House – gold and silver pieces,
Royal orbs, sceptres and crowns and the biggest cut diamond
in the world, the First Star of Africa. The White Tower houses
the Royal Armouries – the largest collection of medieval and
Tudor armour in Britain. The Lower Martin Tower holds instruments of torture and the executioner's block and axe. *Guided
tours by Yeomen Warders every ½ hr (except in bad weather);
last tour 15.30 Mar-Oct; 14.30 Nov-Feb. Open Mar-Oct 09.30-
18.00 Mon-Sat, 10.00-18.00 Sun (last admission 17.00); Nov-
Feb 09.30-17.00 Mon-Sat (last admission 16.00).* Charge.

Victoria & Albert Museum   6 D1
Cromwell Rd SW7. 071-938 8500. National museum of art and
design and the largest decorative arts museum in the world.
An immense and wide-ranging collection; where else can you
see a Raphael cartoon and 1960s designer clothes under one
roof? Advisable to get the booklet *100 Things to See* at the
bookshop to show you round the important exhibits.
Restaurant. Shop. *Open 12.00-17.50 Mon, 10.00-17.50 Tue-
Sun.* Donation welcome.

Wallace Collection   4 B1
Hertford House, Manchester Sq W1. 071-935 0687. A private col-
lection of outstanding works of art which was bequeathed to the
nation by Lady Wallace in 1897. Splendid representation of the
French 17thC and 18thC artists, including paintings by Fragonard,
Watteau and Boucher. Home to the *Laughing Cavalier* by Frans
Hals and also works by Rembrandt, Titian, Rubens, Canaletto and
Guardi. Important collections of French furniture, Sèvres porcelain,
majolica, Limoges enamel and armour. Shop. *Tours by prior
arrangement. Open 10.00-17.00 Mon-Sat, 14.00-17.00 Sun.* Free.

OUT AND ABOUT

London is well-endowed with parks, gardens, commons, forests and heathland. There are over 80 parks within 7 miles of the centre of London – all that remain of early London's natural surrounding countryside. Left by accident, gift, or longsighted social intention, they provide a welcome breathing space. The royal parks are still the property of the Crown and were originally the grounds of royal homes or palaces. All parks are free *to enter, but there may be charges to use the facilities within.*

Parks and open spaces

Alexandra Park

N22. 081-365 2121. 220 acres (90ha) including Alexandra Palace, burnt to the ground six days after it was built in 1873. Rebuilt in 1936, it was again severely damaged by fire in 1980 and is now a multi-purpose entertainments and exhibition centre. Excellent views of the London skyline. Café. Park *open 24 hrs Mon-Sun.* ***Facilities:*** animal enclosure, parkland walk, boating lake, children's playground, conservation area, pitch and putt, playing fields, ski slope.

Battersea Park   6 F5

SW11. 081-871 7530. 200-acre (81ha) park opened 1853 by Queen Victoria. Festival Pleasure Gardens laid out in 1951 to celebrate the Festival of Britain. London Peace Pagoda built 1985 by monks and nuns of the Japanese Buddhist order Nipponzan Myohoji. Based on ancient Indian and Japanese designs, it stands at 110ft (33.5m) and has a double roof. Park *open dawn-dusk.* Playing fields, athletics track, tennis courts *open 08.00-dusk.* ***Facilities:*** all-weather sports surface, athletics track, boating and fishing lake, botanical garden (greenhouse *open 09.30-dusk),* bowling green, children's zoo, deer park, floodlit football pitch, playing fields, tennis.

Blackheath

SE3. 081-854 8888. 275 acres (111.4ha) of open grassland – a prime site for kite-flying and watching the sunset. Good views from all directions, especially Point Hill. The scene for many sporting events. Occasional festivals and fairs at *Easter, spring and late summer Bank hols.* Park *open 24 hrs Mon-Sun.* ***Facilities:*** bowling, cricket, model boat sailing, soccer, tennis.

Facilities: bowling, cricket, model boat sailing, soccer, tennis.

Crystal Palace Park

SE20. 081-778 7148. 70 acres (28.4ha) of park named after Paxton's 1851 Great Exhibition building, moved here from Hyde Park but burnt down in 1936; the vast, impressive ruins still remain. National Youth & Sports Centre opened 1964 with a stadium for 12,000 spectators. In amongst the boating lakes are 20 life-sized replicas of large prehistoric animals. Park *open 08.00-½ hr before dusk Mon-Sun*. *Facilities*: adventure playground, boating and pedalos, children's zoo, circular maze, dry ski slope, fishing, mini fair, mini stream train, ranger guided walks, shire horse cart rides, sports centre.

Green Park   4 C5

SW1. 071-930 1793. No statues or lakes – just 53 acres (22ha) of grass and an abundance of lime, plane and hawthorn trees. Ideal for picnics; a favourite spot for office workers at *lunchtime in summer. Open dawn-dusk Mon-Sun.*

Greenwich Park

SE10. 081-858 2608. A royal park, gaining its royal connections with Henry VIII whose favourite residence was Greenwich Palace (the Royal Naval College now occupies the site). Excellent panoramic views. 200 acres (81ha) with avenues sloping down to the Thames, lined with chestnut trees and 13 acres (5.3ha) of wooded deer park. The National Maritime Museum and the Old Royal Observatory are within the park and the London Marathon starts from here in *spring*. Bandstand used in *summer. Park open Apr-Oct 05.00 (for pedestrians – 07.00 for traffic)-22.00 Mon-Sun; Nov-Mar 07.00-18.00 (or dusk) Mon-Sun. Facilities*: boating pool, children's playground, cricket, rugby, tennis.

Hampstead Heath

(including Kenwood, Golders Hill Park, Parliament Hill) NW3. 071-485 4491. Open and hilly with a feel of real countryside; 800 acres (324ha) of park and woods with fine views of London. Crowded on *Bank hols* with visitors to the famous fair and equally famous pubs, the Bull & Bush, Spaniard's Inn and Jack Straw's Castle. Open-air concerts at Kenwood in *summer*. Parliament Hill, 320ft (110m), is a good spot for kite-flying and excellent views. Heath *open 24 hrs Mon-Sun*. Kenwood and Golders Hill *open dawn-dusk. Facilities*: adventure playground, athletics track, boating and fishing lakes, children's zoo, cricket, football, horse-riding (permit holders only), open-air swimming in several ponds, rounders, rugby, tennis.

Hampton Court & Bushy Park

Surrey. 081-781 9500. 2000 acres (810ha) of royal park, the formal gardens of the great Tudor palace, Hampton Court,

Maze and the Great Vine planted in 1768. **Bushy Park** is natural parkland with an artificial plantation, aquatic plants and ponds. Two herds of deer, fallow and red, roam throughout. Both parks have many fine avenues including the mile-long Chestnut Avenue in Bushy Park. Both parks *open 07.00-dusk Mon-Sun.*

Holland Park   **3 A5**
W8. 071-602 2226. Behind the bustle of Kensington High Street are 55 acres (22.3ha) of calm and secluded lawns and gardens with peacocks, peafowl and pheasants. Once the private garden of Holland House, the Dutch garden dates from 1812 with fine tulip displays, iris and rose gardens, a yucca lawn, Japanese garden and the Orangery. Also a remarkable woodland of 28 acres (11.3ha) containing 3000 species of rare British trees and plants. Open-air theatre in *summer.* Café. Park *open summer 07.30-sunset Mon-Sun; winter 07.30-dusk Mon-Sun.* Restaurant looks out onto Flower Garden which is illuminated at night. *Facilities:* adventure playground, cricket, football, putting green, squash, tennis.

Hyde Park   **3 F4**
W1. 071-262 5484. A royal park since 1536, once part of the forest used by Henry VIII for hunting wild boar and bulls. 360 acres (137.7ha) of parkland, walks, Rotten Row for horse-riders, and the Serpentine – a fine lake, created originally from six ponds, now used for boating and swimming. Serpentine Bridge by George Rennie, 1826. Speakers' Corner, where anyone can speak about anything, is near Marble Arch – public executions were held at the Tyburn gallows, where Marble Arch now stands, until 1783. Baseball and softball are often played. Bandstand used in *summer.* Park *open 05.00-24.00 Mon-Sun.* The Lido *open May-Sep 10.00-18.00 Mon-Sun.* Charge for swimming. *Facilities:* boating lake, children's playground, open-air swimming, tennis.

Kensington Gardens   **3 D4**
W8. 071-724 3104. A formal and elegant addition to Hyde Park. 75 acres (111.4ha) of royal park, containing William III's Kensington Palace, Queen Anne's Orangery, the peaceful 'Sunken Garden', and the Round Pond, perfect for sailing model boats. The Broad Walk, originally flanked by ancient elms, is now replanted with fragrant limes and maples, and the nearby 'Flower Walk' is home to birds such as woodpeckers, flycatchers and tree-creepers. Queen Caroline created both the Long Water (Peter Pan's statue is here) and the Serpentine by ordering the damming of the Westbourne River. Nothing so rowdy as football or cars are allowed here! Café. Park *open dawn-dusk Mon-Sun. Facilities:* children's playground, model boat sailing.

Primrose Hill   **1 B2**
NW8. 112 acres (46.6ha) of open land. Panoramic views over London with a helpful table identifying some of the most prominent landmarks. Popular with duellists in the 19thC, the cleverest battles you'll see now are between kite-flyers. *Open 24 hrs Mon-Sun.*

Regent's Park   **1 C3**
NW1. 071-486 7905. A royal park of 472 acres (191ha), originally part of Henry VIII's great hunting forest in the 16thC. The design (1812-26) by John Nash is of great distinction. It forms two concentric circles – the Inner with gardens and the Outer with Regency terraces and imposing gateways. Here you'll find London Zoo, the Regent's Canal, a fine boating lake with 30 species of bird, a bandstand, fragrant flower gardens and the very fine Queen Mary's Rose Garden. Also home to the golden-domed London Central Mosque. Open-air theatre. Restaurant. Cafés. Park *open 05.00 (or dawn)-dusk Mon-Sun.* **Facilities**: athletics track, baseball, boating lake, children's playgrounds, cricket, football, rugby, tennis.

Richmond Park
Surrey. 081-948 3209. The largest of the royal parks, created by Charles I in 1637. 2358 acres (954.2ha) of natural open parkland with spinneys and plantations, bracken and ancient oaks, and over 600 red and fallow deer. Fine views of the Thames Valley from White Lodge (once a royal residence, now home to the Royal Ballet School). Restaurant and café in Pembroke Lodge. Park *open 07.00 (from 07.30 in winter)-½ hr before dusk Mon-Sun.* **Facilities**: children's playground, fishing (permit needed), football, golf, riding.

St James's Park   **4 E5**
SW1. 071-930 1793. St James's is the oldest royal park, acquired by Henry VIII in 1532 and laid out in imitation 'Versailles' style by Charles II. An attractive setting, with fine promenades and walks, a romantic Chinese-style lake, bridge, and weeping willows. The bird sanctuary on Duck Island has magnificent pelicans and over 20 species of duck and goose. Good views of Buckingham Palace, the domes and spires of Whitehall and, to the south, Westminster Abbey. The Mall and Constitution Hill are frequently part of royal ceremonial occasions. Bandstand used in *summer. Open dawn-dusk Mon-Sun.*

Botanic gardens

Many parks also have living botanical collections. Holland Park has a good arboretum and others have rock gardens and extensive rose gardens, of which Queen Mary Rose Garden in Regent's Park is an outstanding example. The following provide tranquillity in the midst of London:

Chelsea Physic Garden   **6 F4**
Royal Hospital Rd SW3. 071-352 5646. Founded 1673 by the
Worshipful Society of Apothecaries for the collection and study
of plants with medicinal value. Botanical research still carried
out here. Rockery made from Icelandic lava and old stone from
the Tower of London; many fine trees including the biggest
olive tree in Britain – 30ft (9.1m). *Open Apr-Oct 14.00-17.00
Wed & Sun. Other times by appointment only.* Charge.

Museum of Garden History   **7 F1**
St Mary-at-Lambeth, Lambeth Rd SE1. 071-261 1891. 17thC
garden founded at St Mary-at-Lambeth church by the
Tradescants. As gardeners to Charles I and Henrietta Maria,
the father and son team brought many rare plants into this
country, some of which can be seen in the churchyard. *Open
11.00-15.00 Mon-Fri, 10.30-17.00 Sun. Closed Sat.* Free.

Royal Botanic Gardens, Kew
Kew Rd, Richmond, Surrey. 081-940 1171. Superb botanic
gardens of 300 acres (121.5ha), founded in 1759 by Princess
Augusta. Within the grounds are thousands of flowers and
trees plus hot-houses for orchids, palms, ferns, cacti and
alpine plants. Lake and aquatic garden; 10-storey pagoda by
Sir William Chambers (1760); magnificent curved glass Palm
House and Temperate House (1884-8) by Decimus Burton.
The scientific aspect was developed by its two directors, Sir
William and Sir Joseph Hooker. The 17thC Queen's Garden
has a delightful formal rose-bed and the Princess of Wales
Conservatory houses exotic plants. Beneath the Palm
House there is a Marine Display which has examples of
flowering marine plants and coral reef. Café. Gift shop.
Gardens *open from 09.30;* hot-houses *open from 10.00.
Closing times vary according to season – phone in advance
to check.* Charge.

Cemeteries

*London's cemeteries provide a fascinating insight into
Victorian attitudes with their impressive and often idiosyncratic
monuments. Originally privately owned and regimentally planted out, several have since become overgrown and peaceful
sanctuaries for wildlife.*

Brompton   **6 B4**
Old Brompton Rd SW10. Behind busy Fulham Road, vast and full
of ornamental Victorian marble tombs and memorials. Emmeline
Pankhurst, the suffragette, was buried here in 1928. Free.

Highgate
Swain's Lane N6. 081-340 1834. Popular from the first as a
final resting place because of the good views of London from

Highgate West Hill! Winding paths lead up to The Egyptian Avenue and Cedar of Lebanon. Amongst its famous residents are Karl Marx, the writer George Eliot, the actor Sir Ralph Richardson, and the poet Christina Rossetti. Tom Sayers, the bare fisted prizefighter, is guarded by the effigy of his mastiff who was chief mourner at his funeral and attended the ceremony in his own carriage. The conservation of the native woodland and abundance of wild flowers and birds is due to the efforts of the 'Friends of Highgate Cemetery', who offer guided tours *Apr-Sep 12.00, 14.00 & 16.00 Mon-Fri, on the hour 11.00-16.00 Sat & Sun; Oct-Mar 12.00, 14.00 & 15.00 Tue-Fri, on the hour 11.00-15.00 Sat & Sun.* Charge for tours.

Kensal Green
Harrow Rd W10. 081-969 0152. Plenty of admirable monuments and many mature native trees lining the curving avenues. Famous tombs include W.M. Thackeray and Anthony Trollope, Isambard Kingdom Brunel and his father Sir Marc Isambard Brunel, and James Miranda Barry, the Inspector General of the Army Medical Department, who on death was found to be a woman. *Open 09.00-17.30 Mon-Sat, 10.00-17.30 Sun; 10.00-13.00 Bank hols.* Free.

Walking tours

Citisights of London
213 Brooke Rd E5. 081-806 4325. Archaeologists and historians working in association with the Museum of London provide a series of walks and tours looking at the history and archaeology of London. *Phone for details.* Charge.

Historical Walks of London
3 Florence Rd, South Croydon, Surrey. 081-688 4019. Focus on London's history and offer a range of themes from medieval times to the present. Cover areas as diverse as Mayfair and the East End, Hampstead and Docklands. Walks last around *2 hrs*. **Meeting place**: usually at a tube station. *Phone for further details.* Charge.

London Silver Jubilee Walkway
12-mile (19km) walkway created for the Queen's Silver Jubilee in 1977. Circles the centre of London, passing close to many famous and historic buildings. Start at Leicester Square (**4 E3**) and follow the discs set in the pavement. Leaflet obtainable from the London Tourist Board Information Centre, Victoria Station Forecourt SW1 (**7 B2**). 071-730 3488.

London Walks
PO Box 1708 NW6. 071-624 3978. A choice of more than 40 walks lasting about *2 hrs* including Dickens' London, Ghosts of the City and Jack the Ripper haunts. Also pub walks. *Mon-*

Sun; first walk 10.30, last walk 19.30. **Meeting place**: *usually at a tube station. Phone for further details.* Charge.

Streets of London

16 The Grove N3. 081-346 9255. Guided walking tours with a regular programme of scheduled tours, regardless of weather. Themes include Dickens' London and History of London. **Meeting place**: *usually at a tube station. Phone for further details.* Charge.

Coach tours

Cityrama

Silverthorne Rd SW8. 071-720 6663. 20-mile sightseeing tour of all the main London sights. Coaches leave *every 30 mins* and tours take *1-1½ hrs.* Coaches leave from Coventry Street W1 (**4 E3**) and Grosvenor Gdns SW1 (**4 C6**). Also tours to Bath, Stonehenge, Stratford-upon-Avon and Windsor.

Evan Evans   **4 E4**

27 Cockspur St SW1. 071-930 2377. Well-established tour company which operates a variety of tours; *full day, morning* or *afternoon* plus a *2½ hr* general drive around the capital and a *30-min* cruise on the Thames. Also run extended tours out of London.

Harrods   **3 G6**

Sightseeing Tours Dept, 4th Floor, Harrods, Knightsbridge SW1. 071-730 1234. The most luxurious coach tour of London; takes *2 hrs* with a taped commentary in several languages and refreshments on board. Also tours to Stratford-upon-Avon and Blenheim Palace.

Original London Sightseeing Tours

London Coaches, Jew's Row SW18. 081-877 1722. Round London tours in traditional double-decker buses, some of which are open-topped. A great favourite with children. *Phone for further details.*

River trips and tours

One of the best ways to appreciate London is to take a boat trip. The Thames is a fascinatingly beautiful river, particularly as it passes through the city, where the buildings lining its banks conjure up a whole host of historic, artistic and literary associations. Apart from the commuter Riverbus (see page 23), there are several companies running river and canal trips. The London Tourist Board provides an excellent River Trips telephone information service on (0839) 123432 (recorded information).

NB: always check times of return boats at the pier on arrival.

DOWNRIVER SERVICES
Charing Cross Pier   4 F4
Victoria Embankment WC2. 071-839 3572. Trips to the Tower
(20 mins) and Greenwich *(45 mins)* Apr-Oct *every half hour
between 10.30-16.00 Mon-Sun; Nov-Mar every 45 mins
between 10.30-15.00 Mon-Sun.* 2-hr luncheon cruise *12.45
Sun only; all year.*
Greenwich Pier
Return services to Charing Cross Pier *(45 mins)*, Tower Pier
(½ hr) and Westminster Pier *(45 mins)*. *Phone the individual
pier for details.*
Tower Pier   5 F4
071-488 0344. Trips to Greenwich *(½ hr) every half hour 11.00-
17.00 in summer (departures at 10.15, 12.30 and 14.45 Nov-
Mar);* to Westminster *(25 mins) every 20 mins 11.00-18.00 in
summer (every 40 mins 11.00-17.00 Nov-Mar).* Ferry to *HMS
Belfast (5 mins) every 15 mins in summer only.*
Westminster Pier   4 F5
Victoria Embankment WC2. 071-930 4097. Trips to the Tower
(½ hr) every 20 mins 10.30-16.00 and to Greenwich *(50 mins)
every half hour 10.30-16.00; all year.* Special trips to the
Thames Flood Barrier *(1¼ hrs each way) 10.00, 11.15, 12.45,
13.45 & 15.15 Mar-Nov.* Disco cruises *19.00 Fri & 20.00 Sat;
all year.*

UPRIVER SERVICES
Westminster Pier   4 F5
Victoria Embankment SW1. Westminster Passenger Services
operate boat trips *during summer only* to Putney *(½ hr)*, Kew
(1½ hrs), Richmond *(2 hrs)* and Hampton Court *(3-4 hrs). Phone
071-930 2062 for departure times.*
There are local services to Hampton Court from Richmond and
Kingston *(Easter-Sep). Phone 081-546 2434 for details.*

UPPER THAMES
Salter Bros
Follybridge, Oxford. (0865) 243421. Salter's steamers run from
Oxford-Abingdon, Reading-Henley, Maidenhead-Windsor and
Windsor-Staines; *May-Sep Mon-Sun. Phone for details.*

Canal trips

Canal Water Bus   1 D1
London Waterbus Company, Camden Lock Place NW1. 071-
482 2550. Boats leave from Little Venice, stopping at London
Zoo and continuing to Camden Lock; *Apr-Sep 10.00-17.00
Mon-Sun.* Also run Limehouse/River Lea trips which explore

the architecture and industrial history of London's quiet canal-ways; *May-Oct 09.30-18.00 Sat. Phone for details of departure times.*

Jason's Trip   3 C1
opposite 60 Blomfield Rd W9. 071-286 3428. The traditional narrowboat *Jason* leaves Little Venice for a *1½-hr* return trip with commentary, through Regent's Park (with London Zoo) to Camden Lock. Disembark to look round the craft shops if you like, or the market at *weekends*. Refreshments and lunch available. *Phone for details of departure times.*

Jenny Wren Cruises   1 D1
250 Camden High St NW1. 071-485 4433. *Jenny Wren*, a traditional canal boat, goes from Camden Lock to Little Venice without stopping. The round trip takes *1½ hrs*. Trips run from *Feb-Nov four times a day Mon-Sun. Phone for details of departure times.*

Zoos, safari parks and fun days out

Bekonscot Model Village
Warwick Rd, Beaconsfield, Bucks. (0494) 672919. 23 miles/37km west (A40, M40). Miniature wonderland set in the 1930s, created by Roland Callingham. A raised viewing plat-form offers a bird's eye view of the miniature world of shops, streets and inhabitants, but the real home pride of Bekonscot is the model (gauge 1) railway which travels round the village. *Open Mar-Oct 10.00-17.00 Mon-Sun.* Charge.

Birdworld & Underwater World
Holt Pound, Farnham, Surrey. (0420) 22140. 30 miles/48km south west (A3, A31). Situated on the edge of Alice Holt Forest, there are beautiful gardens here which make the per-fect home for a huge variety of birds from the tiny humming bird to the huge ostrich. Watch the pelicans catch fish in their beaks or feeding time at Penguin Island. There are good, well laid-out trails. **Underwater World** is next door, with a large indoor aquarium full of amazing colourful tropical fish. Both *open Apr-Aug 09.30-18.00 Mon-Sun; Sep 09.30-17.00 Mon-Sun; Oct-Mar 09.30-16.00 Mon-Sun.* Charge.

Chessington World of Adventures
Leatherhead Rd, Chessington, Surrey. (0372) 727227. 12 miles/19km south (A3, A243). 65 acres (27ha) comprising a zoo and theme park with wild rides such as Calamity Canyon and The Vampire – Britain's first hanging roller coaster. Visit the Mystic East, Circus World and Toytown. A monorail travels high above the zoo animals. All attractions *open mid Mar-Oct 10.00-17.00 Mon-Sun;* zoo only *open Nov-Mar 10.00-16.00 Mon-Sun.* Charge.

Chislehurst Caves
Old Hill, Chislehurst, Kent. 081-467 3264. 12 miles/19km south east (A2, A20, A222). A maze of chalk tunnels and caves, created in the stone ages. The caves have been inhabited in the past by druids, the Romans and Londoners seeking shelter during the air raids of World War II. Go on one of the eerie lamplight guided tours. They last *45 mins* and leave *every half hour.* On *Sun and Bank hols* there is a *1½-hr* tour which leaves at *14.30. Open 11.00-16.30 Mon-Sun.* Charge.

Cotswold Wildlife Park
Burford, Oxon. (099382) 3006. 75 miles/120km west (M40, A40). Here it's the animals who roam in relative freedom in the 180 acres (75ha) and the public must keep to the carefully controlled walks. Zebras, rhino, deer, wallabies, antelope – they may well come and 'inspect' you! More dangerous species, such as leopards, are caged. Adventure playground and farmyard where tame animals can be stroked. Pony rides. Narrow gauge railway operates *during summer.* Restaurant. Brass rubbing centre. *Open 10.00-18.00 (or dusk) Mon-Sun.* Charge.

London Zoo   1 C3
Regent's Park NW1. 071-722 3333. Famous zoo with a huge collection of animals. Aviary designed by Lord Snowdon. 'Moonlight World' reverses day and night so that rarely-seen nocturnal animals are kept awake during the day. *Open Mar-Oct 10.00-17.30 Mon-Sun; Nov-Feb 10.00-dusk Mon-Sun. Closed Xmas Day.* Charge (includes admittance to London Aquarium).

Thorpe Park
Staines Rd, Chertsey, Surrey. (0932) 562633. 21 miles/34km south west (A308). A wonderful place for all ages, with lots of rides and entertainments such as Space Station Zero and Thunder River. Thorpe Farm is good for small children. All rides covered by entrance fee. *Open end Mar-Jun 10.00-17.00 Mon-Sun; Jul-Sep 10.00-18.00 Mon-Sun; Oct 10.00-17.00; (last admission 2 hours before closing time). Closed Nov-end Mar.* Charge (children under 1 metre tall free!).

Whipsnade Wild Animal Park
Dunstable, Beds. (0582) 872171. 32 miles/51km north (M1, A5). Natural zoo of woods and downland with over 3000 animals in large open-air enclosures. Some species roam freely. Travel round the park by car or aboard the miniature motor coach train. Also a Discovery Centre with hands-on displays, a miniature desert and wall-to-wall rainforests. *Open Apr-Oct 10.00-dusk Mon-Sun; Nov-Mar 10.00-16.00 Mon-Sun.* Charge.

Woburn Wild Animal Kingdom & Leisure Park
Woburn, Beds. (0525 290407. 40 miles/64km north (M1). Britain's largest drive-through safari park. A winding route

takes you past tigers, bears, wolves, rhinos and mischievous monkeys! At the end of the safari trail you can watch sealion and parrot shows. Leisure area with rides, boating lakes and cable car. 3000-acre (1250ha) park surrounding Woburn Abbey contains original herd of Père David deer. *Open mid Mar-end Oct 10.00-17.00 Mon-Sun; Nov-mid Mar 11.00-15.00 Sat & Sun.* Charge.

Stately homes

Arundel Castle

Arundel, W. Sussex. (0903) 883136. 58 miles/93km south (A24, A29). Once an imposing feudal stronghold overlooking the River Arun. Home to the Dukes of Norfolk for 700 years. Magnificent collection of paintings by van Dyck, Holbein and Gainsborough. *Open Apr-Oct 11.00-17.00 Mon-Fri & Sun (closed Sat). Closed Nov-Mar & all Bank hols. Last admission 1 hour before closing time.* Charge.

Blenheim Palace

Woodstock, Oxon. (0993) 811325. 60 miles/96km west (M40, A34). Birthplace of Sir Winston Churchill. Huge palace built 1705-22 by Sir John Vanbrugh. Fine example of English baroque architecture. Now home to the 11th Duke of Marlborough. Fine tapestries, sculpture and furnishings. *Open mid Mar-Oct 10.30-17.30 Mon-Sun. Closed Nov-mid Mar.* Charge.

Goodwood

nr Chichester, W. Sussex. (0243) 774107. 60 miles/96km south (A3, A283, then A285 or A286). 18thC house by James Wyatt. Home to the 10th Duke of Richmond. Superb artistic connections, with masterpieces by Canaletto, van Dyck, Kneller and Reynolds. Fine examples of French furniture, Sèvres porcelain and Gobelins tapestries. House often used for entertainment functions. Aerodrome and famous motor circuit nearby. Has its own race-course, where 'Glorious Goodwood', a famous meet, takes place at the *end of Jul.* Advisable to phone in advance as there is *no public access on event days. Open May-Sep 14.00-17.00 Sun & Mon (also open 14.00-17.00 Tue-Thur in Aug); open Easter Sun & Mon. Closed on event days.* Charge.

Hatfield House

Hatfield, Herts. (0707) 262823. 21 miles/34km north (A1, A1000). Jacobean mansion built 1611 for Robert Cecil, 1st Earl of Salisbury. Still home to the Cecil family. Famous portraits, rare tapestries, fine furniture and armour. Tudor Old Royal Palace in grounds, where Queen Elizabeth I learned of her accession to the throne. Beautiful grounds with woodlands and lake. *Open (guided tours only) end Mar-Oct 12.00-17.00 Tue-Sat, 13.30-17.00 Sun (last tour 16.00). Closed Mon except*

Bank hols; open 11.00-17.00 (no guided tours). Closed Nov-end Mar. Charge.

Leeds Castle

Maidstone, Kent. (0622) 765400. 40 miles/64km south east (A20, M20). Beautiful, romantic, restored castle (AD 857). Magnificent collection of medieval furnishings, French and English fabrics, tapestries and paintings by Degas, Pissarro and Vuillard. Delightful gardens. Shop, café, garden centre. *Open Mar-Oct 11.00-17.00 Mon-Sun; Nov-Feb 10.00-15.00 Mon-Sun (last admission 1 hour before closing time).* Charge.

Royal Pavilion, Brighton

Old Steine, Brighton, E. Sussex. (0273) 603005. 45 miles/72km south (A23). Fantastic Oriental seaside 'villa' with onion domes and minarets built for the Prince Regent (later George IV) by Nash 1815-22. Lavish Chinese-style staterooms. *Open Jun-Sep 10.00-18.00 Mon-Sun; Oct-May 10.00-17.00 Mon-Sun.* Charge.

Windsor Castle

Windsor, Berks. (0753) 868286. 20 miles/32km west (M4). Imposing 800-year-old medieval fortress. 12thC Round Tower built by Henry II; St George's Chapel fine example of 16thC perpendicular. Magnificent State Apartments. St George's Hall and the Grand Reception Room were severely damaged by fire in November 1992. An exhibition in the Waterloo Chamber illustrates the damage caused by the fire and visitors can watch the renovations taking place through perspex screens. *Opening times depend on the movements of the royal family and ceremonial occasions, so check with the Castle Information Office.* Charge for interior.

Woburn Abbey

Woburn, Beds. (0525) 290666. 40 miles/64km north (M1). Home of Dukes of Bedford for over 300 years. Built on the site of a Cistercian monastery, founded 1145. Present building dates from 17thC and 18thC. Set in 3000-acre park, part of which is now a safari park (see page 70). Collection of paintings includes works by Rembrandt, Gainsborough, Holbein and Canaletto. *Open Jan-Mar 11.00-16.00 Sat & Sun; Apr-Oct 11.00-17.00 Mon-Sun. Closed Nov & Dec.* Charge.

Day trips

The telephone numbers listed in the following entries refer to the Tourist Information centre in the town. ⇟ *refers to the British Rail station for that destination.*

Bath

107 miles/171km west (M4, A4). ⇟ : Paddington. (0225) 462831. Elegant Georgian town, rich in architectural detail.

See the dramatic sweeping curve of Ionic columns forming the Royal Crescent. Several museums including Roman Baths with natural hot springs, from which the town got its name and indeed its existence. Good shops.

Brighton

56 miles/90km south (A23). ⇌: Victoria. (0273) 23755. Originally a poor fishing village which became fashionable when the Royal Pavilion was built here (see page 72). Splendid Regency terraces, five miles of beach and interesting shops in The Lanes; unusual jewellery, antiques, clothes and artefacts. The restored Victorian pier is full of attractions. Newly developed marina has waterside pubs and cafés.

Cambridge

60 miles/96km north (M11). ⇌: King's Cross. (0223) 322640. University city of spires, mellow colleges and riverside meadows, bordering the River Cam. Hire a punt to view the university colleges and serene lawns. 31 colleges in total; the oldest, Peterhouse, was established in 1284. King's College Chapel is one of the world's Gothic masterpieces. The Fitzwilliam Museum has a superb collection of classical antiquities and paintings.

Henley-on-Thames

Oxon. 36 miles/57km west (A4). ⇌: Paddington. (0993) 778800. Situated on a very pretty part of the Thames and most famous for the Regatta, held in *early Jul* (see page 50). Arched bridge was built in 1786. In St Mary's churchyard are 16thC almshouses and a rare unspoilt 15thC timber-framed building – the Chantry House. The Regatta is held on the straight mile of river downstream from the bridge.

Oxford

56 miles/90km west (M40). ⇌: Paddington. (0865) 726871. A University city of 'dreaming spires' and fine college buildings. 30 colleges, all worth a visit – the grandest being Christ Church and the oldest University College (1249). Other attractions include the Sheldonian Theatre by Wren, the 15thC Bodleian Library, the Ashmolean Museum, and the oldest botanic gardens in Britain. In addition there are several good pubs and restaurants.

Stratford-on-Avon

Warks. 90 miles/144km north west (M40, A34). ⇌: Liverpool Street. (0789) 293127. The birthplace of William Shakespeare (1564-1616). The town is still Elizabethan in atmosphere, with overhanging gables and timbered inns. Visit the writer's birthplace in Henley Street, his house at New Place, Anne Hathaway's cottage and the museum and picture gallery. The Shakespeare Memorial Theatre in Waterside is thriving and progressive.

SHOPPING

Generally shops open 09.00/10.00-17.30/18.00 Mon-Sat and are closed on Sun & Bank hols. *Many Bond Street shops* do not open on Sat. *In cases where a shop's hours differ from the standard times above, the opening hours appear in* italic *at the end of the entry. Some areas have a late shopping night. See individual shopping areas below.*

Tax free shopping

Most goods and services in the UK are subject to VAT (value added tax) at the standard rate of 17½%. Luxury items – such as tobacco, perfume, alcoholic beverages and motor vehicles – are subject to higher rates. A good way to purchase tax-free goods is to shop in stores showing the London Tax Free Shopping sign. This system entails filling in a voucher, presenting it to customs with the goods and returning it to the London Tax Free Shopping organisation which will then immediately refund your money in the currency of your country of residence.

Shopping areas

Camden   1 D2
A popular and trendy canalside area lined with shops and a huge, sprawling market. Come here if you're looking for period clothes, alternative books, imported records, pine furniture and artefacts. It's at its busiest and liveliest on *Sat & Sun afternoons.*

Covent Garden   4 F3
Once the site of the famous fruit and vegetable market, this is now a fashionable pedestrianised piazza. The arcades are lined with small specialist fashion and gift shops, plus plenty of places to eat and drink. There are also open-air craft stalls, an antiques market and an occasional craft market. Leading off the piazza in every direction, the streets reveal an interesting variety of shops and restaurants with the latest in fashion, high-tech household equipment and exotic foods. *Late night Thur. Many shops* open late Mon-Sat *and* all day Sun.

Kensington High Street   3 B6
Less hectic than Oxford Street, though a similar range of shops and large branches of most high street chains, plus

Aquascutum 734 6090
Army & Navy 834 1234
Asprey 493 6767
Austin Reed 734 6789
BHS (Kensington High St) 937 0919
BHS (Oxford St) 629 2011
Burberrys 930 3343
C & A 629 7272
Cartier 493 6962
Christie's 839 9060
Conran Shop 589 7401
DH Evans 629 8800
Debenhams 580 3000
Dickins & Jones 734 7070
Dillons 636 1577
Fenwick 629 9161
Fortnum & Mason 734 8040
Foyles 437 5660
General Trading Company 730 0411
Habitat (King's Rd) 351 1211
Habitat (Tottenham Court Rd) 631 3880
Hamleys 734 3161
Harrods 730 1234
Harvey Nichols 235 5000
Hatchards 439 9924
Heal's 636 1666
HMV 631 3423
Jaeger 734 8211
John Lewis 629 7711
Laura Ashley 437 9760
Liberty 734 1234
Lillywhites 930 3181
Littlewoods 434 4301
London Pavilion 437 1838
Maples 387 7000
Marks & Spencer (Ken. High St) 938 3711
Marks & Spencer (Marble Arch) 935 7954
Marks & Spencer (Oxford St) 437 7722
Mothercare 629 6621
Next (Kensington High St) 938 4211
Next (Regent St) 434 2515
Peter Jones 730 3434
Plaza on Oxford St 637 8811
Selfridges 629 1234
Simpson 734 2002
Sotheby's 493 8080
Top Shop 636 7700
Tower Records 439 2500
Trocadero 439 1791
Victoria Place Shopping Centre 931 8811
Virgin Megastore 631 1234
Whiteleys Shopping Centre 229 8844

© Nicholson

SHOPPING IN LONDON

Shaded areas denote main shopping streets

Numbers given at main railway stations indicate useful bus transport to shopping areas

Paddington
Ken High St 27
Oxford St 7, 15, 23
Regent St 15, 23
Strand 15, 23
Paddington 15, 23

Marylebone
(buses from Baker St)
Ken High St 27
Oxford St 2B, 13, 74, 82,
113, 139, 159, 274
Regent St 13, 139, 159
Victoria St 2B, 82

Euston
Bromptom Rd 14, 74
Charing Cross Rd 10, 14, 24, 29, 134
Ken High St 10, 27
Knightsbridge 10, 14, 74
Oxford St 10, 14, 24, 29, 73, 134, 135
Piccadilly 14
Strand 30, 168, 188
Victoria 24, 73

King's Cross & St Pancras
Bromptom Rd 10, 14, 74
Charing Cross Rd 10, 14, 14A, 73
High Holborn 17, 45, 46
Ken High St 10
Knightsbridge 10, 14, 73, 74
Oxford St 10, 14, 14A, 24, 73
Strand 30, 168, 188
Victoria 24, 73

Liverpool St
Charing Cross Rd 8, 11, 22B, 23
High Holborn 8, 22B
King's Rd 11
Oxford St 23
Piccadilly 23
Strand 11, 23, 26, 505
Victoria St 11

Cannon St
High Holborn 17, 521
King's Rd 11
Oxford St 11
Strand 11, 15, X15, 23, 26, 76, 521
Tottenham Court Rd 176
Victoria St 11

Charing Cross
Bond St 176
Charing Cross Rd 24
Ken High St 9, 10
Knightsbridge 9
Oxford St 6, 13, 15, 23, 94,
139, 159

Waterloo
Charing Cross Rd 176
High Holborn 1, 68, X68, 171, 188, 501, 505, 521
King's Rd 11
Strand 1, 4, 26, X68, 76, 171, 171A, 176, 188, 501, 505, 521
Tottenham Court Rd 176
Victoria St 507, 511

Victoria
Bond St 8, 73
Charing Cross Rd 24
Ken High St 52
King's Rd 11
Knightsbridge 52

Victoria Place Shopping Centre
Oxford St 38
Strand 11
Tottenham Court Rd 24

Barkers of Kensington, its own department store. Delve into the roads leading off for more individual (and more expensive) fashion shops. *Late night Thur.*

King's Road/Chelsea   6 E3

Still as much a place to be seen in as to see, this area really comes alive on *Sat* with the parading trendies outdoing each other in outrageousness. One of the centres for up-to-the-minute fashion, plus high street chains, it is particularly good for shoes and men's clothing. *Late night Wed.*

Knightsbridge   3 G5

A traditionally fashionable area for the rich and famous, dominated by Harrods and Harvey Nichols. Beauchamp Place also has exclusive furniture, jewellery and clothes. *Late night Wed.*

Piccadilly/Trocadero/London Pavilion   4 E3

Quality and tradition in the form of Fortnum & Mason, Hatchards, Simpson, and Lillywhites. Also the historic Burlington Arcade. The Trocadero and London Pavilion cater for the more up-to-date taste with one-stop shopping, refreshment and entertainment, while Tower Records dominates Piccadilly Circus from the old Swan & Edgar building. Many shops *open late Mon-Sat.*

Soho   4 E2

Much less sleazy, but as cosmopolitan as ever, Soho is an excellent location for specialist shopping. International food shops, oriental supermarkets, and designer clothes. Also trendy restaurants and wine bars. Berwick Street Market and Chinatown both merit a visit.

West End

London's biggest shopping area consisting of three main streets. **Oxford Street (4 C2)** is over a mile long and has nearly all the major department stores including Selfridges, John Lewis, London's largest Marks & Spencer and an overwhelming assortment of individual fashion shops. It gets very crowded here, especially on *Sat* and at *lunchtime*. **Regent Street (4 D3)** is less hectic and offers luxurious items and gifts at Liberty, plus several china, glass and clothing stores and the department store Dickins & Jones. **Carnaby Street (4 D3)** is still worth a visit. World-renowned in the 1960s, it has retained its busy and lively atmosphere, with frequent pavement shows and interesting clothes and souvenir shops. Some of the high street chains have now also moved in. For real luxury try **New Bond Street (4 C3)** where you'll find shoes, jewellery, prints, pictures and designer clothes. Two pedestrianised streets just off Oxford Street, and well worth exploring, are **St Christopher's Place (4 B2)** and **South Molton Street (4 C2)**. Both are packed with stylish small shops and attractive eating places. *Late night Thur.*

Whiteleys 3 C3

Queensway W2. One of the first department stores, now transformed into a smart, cosmopolitan complex of shops, cafés, restaurants, bars and an eight-screen cinema. Many shops *open late Mon-Sat.*

Department stores

Army & Navy 7 C1

101-105 Victoria St SW1. 071-834 1234. Excellent food hall and wine department. Clothing, cosmetics, household goods, toys, books, china and glass. Hairdressing salon. Coffee shop. Restaurant. *Open 09.30-18.00 Mon-Sat (to 19.00 Thur).*

Barkers of Kensington 3 C5

63 Kensington High St W8. 071-937 5432. Fashionable clothes, household and electrical goods and a hairdressing/beauty salon. Restaurant. Café. *Open 10.00-18.30 Mon-Fri (to 19.30 Thur), 09.30-18.30 Sat.*

BHS (British Home Stores) 4 C2

252 Oxford St W1. 071-629 2011. Inexpensive clothes and accessories for men, women and children. Household goods and extensive lighting department. Restaurant. *Open 09.00-19.00 Mon-Sat (to 20.00 Thur).*

Debenhams 4 D2

344-348 Oxford St W1. 071-580 3000. Fashion clothes at reasonable prices. Good kitchenware, lingerie, hosiery and cosmetics departments. Restaurant. *Open 09.00-19.00 Mon & Tue, 10.00-20.00 Wed, 09.30-20.00 Thur & Fri, 09.30-19.00 Sat.*

D.H. Evans 4 D2

318 Oxford St W1. 071-629 8800. Part of the House of Fraser group with excellent fashion and lingerie departments. Unusual sizes are well catered for in the dress department. Also perfumery, furniture and household goods. Astral Sports is in the basement. Restaurant. Café. *Open 10.00-18.30 Mon-Fri (to 20.00 Thur), 09.00-19.00 Sat.*

Dickins & Jones 4 D3

224 Regent St W1. 071-734 7070. Fashionable store selling stylish ladies' and men's clothes, accessories and haberdashery. Excellent and wide range of dress fabrics. Also china and glass departments. Hairdressers. Beauty salon. Restaurant. Coffee shop. *Open 09.30-18.00 Mon-Sat (to 20.00 Thur).*

Fenwicks 4 C3

63 New Bond St W1. 071-629 9161. Good fashions and accessories. Imaginative gifts and stationery and a wide selection of books. *Open 09.30-18.00 Mon-Sat (to 19.30 Thur).*

Fortnum & Mason 4 D4

181 Piccadilly W1. 071-734 8040. Well-established and

respected store. Famous for its exotic foods, but also offers jewellery, china, glass, fashion, perfumery, leather goods, toys, stationery and a beauty salon. Two restaurants. Tea room. *Open 09.00-18.00 Mon-Sat.*

Harrods   3 G6
Knightsbridge SW1. 071-730 1234. The world's most famous department store – over 60 fashion departments with men's, ladies' and children's clothing and accessories. Also perfumes, gifts, china, glass, pets, toys, books, furniture and fabrics. The Edwardian marble food halls are well worth a visit for their luxury foods. Wide range of services. Bureau de change. Barber's shop. Hairdressers. Beauty salon. Six restaurants. Three coffee shops. *Open 10.00-18.00 Mon, Tue & Sat, 10.00-19.00 Wed, Thur & Fri.*

Harvey Nichols   4 A5
Knightsbridge SW1. 071-235 5000. Elegant, stylish clothes from top British, Continental and American designers. Home furnishings and household goods. Restaurant. *Open 10.00-19.00 Mon-Fri, to 18.00 Sat.*

Heal's/Habitat   4 E1
196 Tottenham Court Rd W1. 071-631 3880. Terence Conran's brainchild – Habitat offers affordable furniture, kitchenware, rugs, stationery, posters. Heal's is more expensive with more unusual designs and gift ideas. Restaurant. *Open 09.30-18.00 Mon-Sat (to 19.30 Thur).*

John Lewis   4 C2
278-306 Oxford St W1. 071-629 7711. One of the largest dress fabric departments in Europe, as well as furniture, furnishings, china, glass, household goods and fashions. Excellent haberdashery department. Bureau de change. Interpreters available. NB: They do not take credit cards. Restaurant. Coffee shop. Other branches. *Open 09.00-17.30 Mon-Sat (09.30-20.00 Thur).*

Liberty   4 D3
210-220 Regent St W1. 071-734 1234. Famous and fashionable, well-known for distinctive fabrics and unusual luxury goods. Good selection of unusual jewellery and rare gifts, plus glass, china, oriental rugs, prints, gifts and several designer-label collections. Restaurant. Coffee shop. *Open 09.30-18.00 Mon-Sat (to 19.30 Thur).*

Littlewoods   4 B2
508-520 Oxford St W1. 071-629 7847. Inexpensive high street chain for clothing and household goods. *Open 09.00-19.00 Mon-Sat (to 20.00 Thur).*

Marks & Spencer   4 B2
458 Oxford St W1. 071-935 7954. Well-loved chain with good quality inexpensive clothing and accessories for men, women

and children. Wide range of foods, home furnishings, cosmetics and gifts. Other branches. Bureau de change. NB: They do not take credit cards. *Open 09.00-19.00 Mon-Wed & Sat, to 20.00 Thur & Fri.*

Peter Jones   **6 F2**
Sloane Sq SW1. 071-730 3434. (Part of same chain as John Lewis.) Excellent quality and good value clothing, accessories and household goods. Also modern and antique furniture, glass, china, and a large furnishing fabric department. Interpreters available. Restaurant. Coffee shop. NB: They do not take credit cards. *Open 09.00-17.30 Mon-Sat (09.30-19.00 Wed).*

Selfridges   **4 B2**
400 Oxford St W1. 071-629 1234. Vast store with huge range of clothing, accessories and household goods. Also toys, sports clothing and equipment and an impressive food hall. Three restaurants. Five cafés. *Open 09.30-19.00 Mon-Sat (to 20.00 Thur).*

Clothes stores

Nearly all London's department stores have extensive collections of clothes and accessories, but these are the specialists:

Aquascutum   **4 D3**
100 Regent St W1. 071-734 6090. Fine quality British raincoats, coats, suits, knitwear and accessories for men and women.

Austin Reed   **4 D3**
103 Regent St W1. 071-734 6789. English and Continental suits and accessories for men. Accent on quality. Valet service and barber. Also ladies' clothing, executive suits, designer wear and classic dresses.

Burberrys   **4 E3**
18 Haymarket SW1. 071-930 3343. Classic raincoats for men and women cut in the English style. Hats, scarves, suits and accessories. Other branches.

C&A   **4 B2**
501-509 Oxford St W1. 071-629 7272. Vast selection of reasonably priced fashions and classics for all the family including skirts, dresses, coats, knitwear, suits and leathers. Clockhouse is for 14-25 year-olds. Good selection of sports clothing, especially ski wear. Other branches. *Open 09.30-19.00 Mon-Sat (to 20.00 Thur).*

Jaeger   **4 D3**
200-206 Regent St W1. 071-734 8211. Four floors of well-cut, fashionable English clothes. Suits, coats, knitwear and casual wear for men; dresses, suits and separates for women in colour co-ordinated departments. Accessories, jewellery, perfumes and Italian footwear. Other branches.

Conversion charts

Clothing Sizes
In London you will find English, Continental and American sizing in clothes shops, whereas there is a combination of English and Continental sizing for shoes.

Dresses

English	10	12	14	16	18	20	22
	32	**34**	**36**	**38**	**40**	**42**	**44**
USA	8	10	12	14	16	18	20
Continental	38	40	42	44	46	48	50

Shoes

English	3	$3\frac{1}{2}$	4	$4\frac{1}{2}$	5	$5\frac{1}{2}$	6	$6\frac{1}{2}$	7	$7\frac{1}{2}$	8
USA	$4\frac{1}{2}$	5	$5\frac{1}{2}$	6	$6\frac{1}{2}$	7	$7\frac{1}{2}$	8	$8\frac{1}{2}$	9	$9\frac{1}{2}$
Continental	35	36	37	37	38	38	39	40	40	41	41

Hats

English	$6\frac{5}{8}$	$6\frac{3}{4}$	$6\frac{7}{8}$	7	$7\frac{1}{8}$	$7\frac{1}{4}$	$7\frac{3}{8}$	$7\frac{1}{2}$	$7\frac{5}{8}$
USA	$6\frac{1}{4}$	$6\frac{7}{8}$	7	$7\frac{1}{8}$	$7\frac{1}{4}$	$7\frac{1}{2}$			
Continental	54	55	56	57	58	59	60	61	62

Glove sizes are international.

Weights and Measures

Feet/Metres

English	1	2	3	4	5	6	7	8	9	10
Continental	0.3	0.6	0.9	1.2	1.5	1.8	2.1	2.4	2.7	3.0

Pounds/Kilograms

English	1	2	3	4	5	6	7	8	9	10
Continental	0.4	0.9	1.4	1.8	2.3	2.7	3.2	3.6	4.1	4.5

Pints/Litres

English	$\frac{1}{4}$	$\frac{1}{2}$	$\frac{3}{4}$	1	2	3	4	5
Continental	0.1	0.3	0.4	0.6	1.1	1.7	2.3	2.8

Lillywhites 4 E3
Piccadilly Circus W1. 071-930 3181. Five floors of sports clothing and equipment for just about any sport you can think of.
Moss Bros 4 F3
27-29 King St WC2. 071-240 4567. Men's ceremonial and formal wear. Morning suits, dinner jackets, bow ties, top hat and tails, accessories. Arrange hire at least one week in advance. Deposit required. Other branches.
Next 4 C2
325 Oxford St W1. 071-491 4059. Fashions for men, women and children. Also cosmetics, lingerie, accessories, flowers and home furnishings. Other branches.
Simpson 4 D4
203 Piccadilly W1. 071-734 2002. High-quality clothing for men and women. Shirts, knitwear, dresses and separates. Daks country clothes, luggage and accessories. Restaurant.

Antiques

Good hunting grounds are the King's Road, Portobello Road, Camden Passage in Islington, Kensington Church Street, Fulham Road and Camden Town.

Antiquarius 6 E3
137 King's Rd SW3. 071-352 7989. Over 150 stalls with clothing, jewellery, china, glass, books and prints.
Chelsea Antiques Market 6 E4
245-253 King's Rd SW3. 071-352 5581. Large, busy market – period clothing, watches, books, clocks, prints and scientific instruments.
Gallery of Antique Costume & Textiles
2 Church St NW8. 071-723 9981. Suppliers of antique costumes and textiles including clothing and fabrics from all over the world. Reasonable prices.
Grays Antiques Market 4 C3
1-7 Davies Mews W1. 071-629 7034. Two huge Victorian warehouses with wide selection of antiques – luggage, leather goods, toys, games and jewellery.

Auctioneers

W.& F.C. Bonham & Sons 3 F6
Montpelier Galleries, Montpelier St SW7. 071-584 9161. Paintings, furniture, carpets, porcelain, jewellery and silver. Branch: 65-69 Lots Rd SW10. 071-351 7111.
Christie's 4 D4
8 King St SW1. 071-839 9060. Internationally famous. Comprehensive fine art auctioneers since 1766. Free estimates. Branch: 85 Old Brompton Rd SW7. 071-581 7611.

Sotheby's   **4 C3**
34-35 New Bond St W1. 071-493 8080. Internationally famous for antiques and works of art. Paintings, ceramics, glass, furniture, silver, jewellery, books and manuscripts.

Books

Dillons   **1 F6**
82 Gower St W1. 071-636 1577. Vast stock of paperbacks and hardbacks with large academic range including scientific and language books. Other branches. *Open 09.30-22.00 Mon-Sat, 11.00-19.30 Sun.*

Foyles   **4 E2**
119-125 Charing Cross Rd WC2. 071-437 5660. London's largest book store with practically every English book in print.

Hatchards   **4 D4**
187 Piccadilly W1. 071-439 9921. Something of an institution with a comprehensive selection of general books and knowledgeable staff.

W.H. Smith   **6 F2**
36 Sloane Sq SW1. 071-730 0351. Well-known retailer, with a wide choice of books, magazines, stationery, records, tapes, CDs and games. Many other branches.

Waterstone's   **3 C5**
193 Kensington High St W8. 071-8432. Excellent general store with comprehensive selections in just about every subject you can think of. *Open 09.30-22.00 Mon-Fri, to 19.00 Sat, 11.00-18.00 Sun.*

Crafts

Contemporary Applied Arts   **4 F2**
43 Earlham St WC2. 071-836 6993. Comprehensive display of work by craftsmen using a variety of materials. Many British pieces.

Naturally British   **4 F3**
13 New Row WC2. 071-240 0551. High-quality hand-made British goods including pottery, toys, gifts, clothes, hand-knits and jewellery.

Food

Fortnum & Mason, Harrods and Selfridges have particularly impressive food halls. The following are more specialist shops:

H.R. Higgins   **4 D4**
79 Duke St W1. 071-629 3913. Over 40 types of coffee including original and blended, light, medium and dark roasts.

Hobbs & Co   **4 B3**
29 South Audley St W1. 071-409 1058. Gourmet food and

drink: cheeses, pâtés, wines, pâtisserie, preserves and condiments, fruit and vegetables.

Paxton & Whitfield   **4 D4**
93 Jermyn St W1. 071-930 0259. Over 250 superb English and Continental cheeses plus traditional hams, home-made pies and pâtés.

Gifts

Covent Garden General Store   **4 F3**
111 Long Acre WC2. 071-240 0331. Well-established shop selling a huge range of tasteful gifts including pottery, comestibles, caneware and ornaments. *Open 10.00-23.00 Mon-Wed, 10.00-24.00 Thur-Sat, 11.00-21.00 Sun.*

Crabtree & Evelyn   **3 B4**
6 Kensington Church St W8. 071-937 9335. Exquisite perfumes and toiletries for men and women. All beautifully packaged. *Open 09.30-18.00 Mon-Sat (to 19.00 Thur).*

General Trading Company   **6 F2**
144 Sloane St SW1. 071-730 0411. Some of the best designs in contemporary English and Continental glass and china. Café. *Open 09.00-17.30 Mon-Sat (to 19.00 Wed).*

Markets

Berwick Street   **4 E2**
W1. Busy and boisterous general market in the heart of Soho since 1892. Good value fruit and vegetables; also meat, cheeses, fresh fish and household goods. *Open 09.00-18.00 Mon-Sat.*

Camden Lock   **1 D1**
Where Chalk Farm Rd crosses Regent's Canal NW1. Among the cobbled courtyards and warehouses of the lock is a huge market area selling everything from designer clothes and pine furniture to antique clothing and junk. Also interesting food stalls. *Open 08.00-18.00 Mon-Sun.*

Petticoat Lane   **5 F1**
The name given to the market radiating from Middlesex Street. Probably named after the second-hand clothes dealers who had their businesses here in the early 1600s. Lively and hectic, with mainly clothing on sale, but also toys, food, toiletries and luxury goods. *Open 07.00-14.00 Sun only.*

Portobello Road   **3 A2**
W11. Well-known and much-frequented market extending into Golborne Road and Westbourne Grove. Fruit, vegetables and new goods sold *07.00-18.00 Mon-Sat. Closed Thur.* Second-hand junk and bric-à-brac sold *08.00-17.00 Fri*, and the famous antiques market is held *08.00-17.00 Sat.*

Oxford Street

Left side	No.		No.	Right side
				Charing Cross Road
Fashion M **Hornes**	4		7	**Coles** Fashion M
Pub **The Tottenham**	6		⊖	Tottenham Court Road
Restaurant **McDonald's**	8		15	**K Shoes** Shoes FM
Sock Shop	10		17	**Wigwam** Gifts
Mecca Entertainment & Catering	12		19	Regent School of Languages
Records **Virgin Megastore**	14		19	Office Angels Employment agency
MGM Cinema	16		19	Challoner Employment agency
Comics & books **Virgin**	22		19	**Dillons** Books
Souvenirs **Cerex**	24		25	**Messrs C** Foods
Records, CDs & cassettes **Virgin Megastore**	26		27	**Tandy** Electronics
Sotheby's Library & Educational Services	30		29	Pizza Hut Restaurant
Lloyds Bank	32		33	**Nick Nack** Gifts
Shoes FM **Barratts**	36		35	**Papagallo's** Take-away food
Fashion FM **Jeans Week**	38		37	**Ryman** Stationery
National Westminster Bank	40		41	**Cardshops** Cards & posters
Fashion & bags **Opened**	44		43	Chequepoint Bureau de change
Natural beauty products **Eternité**	46		45	**John Kent** Fashion M
Restaurant **Angus Steak House**	48		45	Mayfair School of English
			47	Key Employment agency
			47	**Sonico Jeans Centre** Fashion FM
			49	**Outlet 49** Fashion M
			49	Kelly Employment agency
			51	**The Bootstore**
Hanway Street			53	**Mondo Pelle** Leather fashion
			55	**Suits You** Fashion M
Shoes M **Footsie 100**	50			
Midland Bank	52			**Soho Street**
			61	**Ratners** Jewellers
Rathbone Place			63	Chequepoint Bureau de change
			65	LIA Amusement Arcade
Fashion FM **Lace**	58		67	**CJ's** Fashion M
Building society **Halifax**	60		73	**Mash** Fashion M
Natural beauty products **The Body Shop**	66		75	**Avirex USA** Fashion M
Handbags **Salisburys**	68a		83	**79 Club** Nightclub
			85	**Exclusive Leather Wear** Fashion FM
Perry's Place			87	**Marmalade** Fashion F
			89	Pizza Hut Restaurant
Hi-fi **McDonalds Electronics**	70		89	**Sock Shop**
Newsagent, gifts & cards **Oxford News**	78			
Computer games **Microbyte**	80			**Dean Street**
Shoes FM **Dolcis**	82			
Cameras & electronics **Dixons**	86		91	**Tie Rack** Fashion FM
			93	**Knickerbox** Underwear
			95	**Eurochange** Bureau de change
			97	**Woodhouse** Fashion M
			101	**Cerex** Souvenirs
Newman Street				
				Great Chapel Street
Opticians **For Eyes**	92		103	**Slot Machine** Fashion FM
Chemist **Boots**	94		105	Sendean Camera repairs
Virgin Games Centre	100		107	London Executive Briefcase Centre
Nightclub **100 Club**	100		107	**Silverdale** Travel goods
Fashion F **Stirling Cooper**	104		109	**Mark-One** Fashion F
National Westminster Bank	112		111	**Cobra** Sports goods
			113	**Bust Clothing Company** Fashion FM
			115	**Warrior** Fashion M
			117	**Athena** Posters, cards, gifts
			117	**Claude Gill** Books
			121	**Skin Image** Fashion F
Berners Street				
				Wardour Street
Fashion F **Principles**	114		127	**Instyle** Clothing Fashion FM & gifts
Fashion M **High & Mighty**	116		129	**Bobtails** Hairdressing salon
Fashion FM **Tie Rack**	118		129	**That's Entertainment** Videos
SHOPPING CENTRE THE PLAZA			137	**Footsie 100** Shoes FM
Fashion FM **Longpoint Bay**	120		139	Callan School of English
Fashion FM **The Gap**	124		141	**Rush Me** Fashion F
			143	**Baloughi** Souvenirs
Wells Street				
				Berwick Street
Sportswear **Olympus**	134		145	**J. D. Sports** Sportswear
Fashion M **Mister Byrite**	140		145	Accountants on Call Employment agency
Restaurant **Burger King**	142		147	**Sacha/Red or Dead** Shoes FM
Novelties, cards **Cascade**	146		147	**Cornet Travel**
Employment agency **Action Secretary**	146		149	**Birthdays** Cards and gifts
Records **HMV Shop**	150		151	Workflow Employment agency
Fashion M **Oakland**	156		151	**Boots** Chemist
Fashion FM **California Jeans**	158		153	**Jane Norman** Fashion F
Fashion M **Profile**	160		155	**The Sale** Fashion FM
Fashion M **Review**	162		159	**Shellys** Shoes
				Poland Street
			163	**Books Etc** Books
			165	Abbey National Building society
			167	**H.Samuel** Jewellers
			173	**MARKS & SPENCER** STORE
			175	**Saxone** Shoes FM
Winsley Street			181	Next Employment agency
			181	**Dolcis** Shoes FM
			185	Ecco Recruitment consultants
			185	**McDonald's** Restaurant
Fashion M **Blazer**	170		187	**Bankrupt Clothing Co** Fashion FM
Sportswear **Champion**	172		189	**Next** Fashion FM
Fashion F **Richards**	174			
Baby store **Mothercare**	174			
Fashion FM **Mark-One**	178			**Ramilles Street**
Great Titchfield Street				
			199	**Leslie Davis** Jewellers
Shoes FM **Ravel**	184		201	**Paperchase** Gifts
Sock Shop	190		213	**LITTLEWOODS** STORE
Shoes FM **Faith**	192		217	**Wallis** Fashion F
Midland Bank	196		219	**Ratners** Jewellers
STORE **C&A**	202			

Oxford Street continued

Great Portland Street | **Hills Place**

Left	No.	No.	Right
Restaurant **Burger King**	214	221	**Miss Selfridge** Fashion F
Fashion **Snob**	216	225	**Benetton** Fashion FM
Fashion F **Evans**	218	227	**Splash** Souvenirs
Fashion FM **Peter Brown**	220	231	**Jeans West** Fashion FM
Fashion M **Burton**	222	233	**The Byrite Company** Fashion M
		235	**Thomas Cook** Bureau de change

Argyll Street

Left	No.	No.	Right
STORE **TOP SHOP & TOP MAN**	214-216	241	**Exchange International** Bureau de change
		266	**Shellys** Shoes FM

Oxford Circus ⊖ **Regent Street**

Fashion F **Hennes**	238	251	**South African Airways**
		257	**Sock Shop**
John Prince's Street		261	**For Eyes** Opticians
		263	**Richards** Fashion F
Fashion M **Mister Byrite**	244	267	**J. D. Sports** Sportswear
Shoes FM **Bally**	246	271	**Croissant Francais** Take-away food
Shoes FM **Ravel**	248	273	**Scottish Woollens** Fashion, knitwear
Jewellers **H. Samuel**	250	275	**Salvation Army Hall**
STORE **BHS**	252	277	**Ernest Jones** Jewellers
Shoes FM **Clarks**	260	283	**River Island** Fashion FM
Fashion F **Jane Norman**	262	287	**Cecil Gee** Fashion M
Fashion F **Kookai**	264	289	**The Deep Pan Pizza Co** Restaurant
Fashion M **Dash**	266	291	**Bureau de change**
Natural beauty products **The Body Shop**	268	291	**Mr Howard** Fashion M
Greetings cards **Clinton**	270	291	**Genel** Fashion M
Fashion F **Wallis**	272	291b	**McDonald's** Restaurant

Holles Street | **Harewood Place**

STORE **JOHN LEWIS**	273-306	293	**Accessorize** Accessories
		295	**Tie Rack** Fashion FM
		297	**Saxone** Shoes FM
		299	**Babers** Shoes M
		299	**City Centre Bureaux** Employment agency
		299	**Noel** Nursing agency
		301	**Olympus Sports** Sports goods and sportswear
		303	**Burton** Fashion M
Old Cavendish Street		309	**Dorothy Perkins** Fashion F
		309	**Swatch** Watches
STORE **D.H. EVANS**	318	315	**Acme** Employment agency
		315	**The Gap** Fashion FM, childrenswear

Chapel Place | **Dering Street**

Shoes FM **K Shoes**	324	321	**Stefanel** Fashion F
Sock Shop	326	321	**Berlitz School of Languages**
Fashion FM **Benetton**	328	321	**Next** Fashion M
Smokers' materials **Bond's**	328	325	**Next** Fashion F
Bank of Scotland	332		

Vere Street | **New Bond Street**

STORE **DEBENHAMS**	344-348	333	**Dolcis** Shoes FM
		335	**Splash** Souvenirs
		337	**Bonjour Paris** Take-away food
		339	**Bureau de change**
		347	**Cafe Zeynah** Take-away food
		341	**Wendy's** Restaurant

Marylebone Lane | **Woodstock Street**

Ties, shirts **Off The Cuff**	350	351	**Le Croissant** Take-away food
Telephones **British Telecom Shop**	350	353	**Thorntons** Chocolates
TSB Bank	350	353	**Brook Street** Employment agency
Marylebone Lane		355	**Scottish Woollens** Fashion FM
		357	**Selection** Fashion FM
Souvenirs **Cerex**	354		
Fashion FM **Oddball Clothing Co**	356		**Sedley Place**
National Westminster Bank	358	359	**Churchill** Gifts
		361	**Oakland** Fashion M
		363	**HMV Shop** Records
		369	**La Brioche Dorée** Take-away food
		369a	**Foreign Exchange Corporation**
	⊖		**Bond Street**
		373	**Leslie Davis** Jewellers

Stratford Place | **Davies Street (South Molton Street)**

Shoes FM **Lilley & Skinner**	360	379	**Top Shop & Top Man** Fashion FM
Fashion F **Kookai**	362	379	**WEST ONE SHOPPING CENTRE**
Fashion M **Woodhouse**	364	383	**Faith** Shoes F
Jewellers **H. Samuel**	366	385	**Boots** Chemist
		393	**Coles** Fashion M
St Christopher's Place		395	**The Gap** Fashion FM
Shoes FM **Bally**	368		
Fashion M **Suits You**	370		
Natural beauty products **The Body Shop**	372		

James Street | **Gilbert Street**

STORE **C&A**	376	399	**Pizzaland** Restaurant
		399	**Lloyds Bank**

Bird Street | **Binney Street**

Shoes FM **Instep Sports**	396	407	**David Clulow** Opticians
Fashion F **Jane Norman**	388	409	**Bertie** Shoes FM
Shoes FM **Barratts**	388	409	**Review** Fashion M
		411	**Kelly Temporary services** Employment agency
		413	**National Westminster Bank**

Left (address)	No.		No.	Right (address)
		Duke Street		**Duke Street**
			415	**Horne Brothers** Fashion M
			419	**Principles** Fashion FM
		Lumley Street		**Lumley Street**
			427	**Samuel Maynard** China & gifts
			429	**Burger King** Restaurant
		Balderton Street		**Balderton Street**
STORE **SELFRIDGES**	400		431	Midland Bank
			435	**Sock Shop**
			439	**Boots** Chemist
			443	British Nursing Association
			443	**Churchill** Gifts
			445	**London House** Fashion FM
			447	**Grip** Fashion M
			449	**Jean Jeanie** Fashion FM
			451	**Laura Ashley** Fashion F
		Orchard Street / **North Audley Street**		
STORE **MARKS & SPENCER**	458		455	**American Burger** Restaurant
National Westminster Bank	466		461	**Mothercare** Baby store
Shoes FM **Bally**	468		467	**Office** Shoes FM
Jewellers **H. Samuel**	472		469	**Knickerbox** Underwear
Shoes FM **Clarks**	476		471	**British Woollen Centre** Fabrics M & tailor
Fashion F **Etam**	484		473	**Jacadi** Childrenswear
Chemist **Boots**	488		473	**Adams** Childrenswear
Shoes FM **Russell & Bromley**	494		479	**Aberdeen Steak House** Restaurant
Sportswear **Bernards**	498		481	**Hennes** Fashion F
Watches of Switzerland	500		483	**Oakland** Fashion M
Shoes FM **Saxone**	502		485	**London Jean Company** Fashion FM
			487	Alfred Marks Employment agency
			487	**Tie Rack** Fashion FM
			489	**Bay Trading Co** Fashion M
			491	**Ryman** Stationery
			493	**Dixons** Cameras & electronics
		Park Street		
STORE **LITTLEWOODS**	506		505	**C&A** STORE
Fashion FM **Benetton**	522		523	**Pizza Hut** Restaurant
Novelty goods **Cascade**	524		525	**Stox** Nick-nacks
Fashion F **Next**	526		527	**Virgin Records** Records, CDs & cassettes
Travel goods **Salisburys**	530		537	**Cerex** Souvenirs
Fashion F **Wallis**	532			
Fashion F **Evans**	538			
		Old Quebec Street		
Restaurant **Kentucky Fried Chicken**	542			**Park Lane**
Bureau de change **Chequepoint**	548			
		Marble Arch ⊖		
Bureau de change **Berkeley Credit**	550			
Cumberland Hotel	552			
China & glass **Chinacraft**	556			
Great Cumberland Place				**Marble Arch**

Bond Street – new and old

Left (address)	No.		No.	Right (address)
Oxford Street				**Oxford Street**
Shoes FM **Dolcis**	87		325	**Next** Fashion F
Fashion M **Blazer**	90		81	**Berkertex Brides** Bridalwear
Fashion M **Cecil Gee**	92		77	**Bambino** Childrenswear
Restaurant **de Lucia**	94		76	**Cerruti 1881** Fashion M
Shoes FM **Grant**	94			
Blenheim Street				**Dering Street**
Shoes F **Kurt Geiger**	95		75	**Cerruti 1881** Fashion M
Royal Bank of Scotland	97		74	**Alexander Juran** Oriental carpets
Linens **Frette**	98		74	**Paul Kaye** Portrait photographer
Employment agency **Manpower**	98		73	**Louis Feraud** Fashion F
Antique restoration **Paul Mitchell**	99		72	**Timberland** Fashion M
Shoes FM **Alan McAfee**	100		71	**Etienne Aigner** Luxury goods, fashion F
Auctioneers **Phillips**	101		70	**Episode** Fashion F
Jewellers **Nawbar & Co**	102		70	**Kabaret** Bar
Leather goods **Henry's**	103		69	**Please Mum** Childrenswear
Shoes F **Ivory**	104		68	**Carvela** Shoes F
Employment agency **Reed**	104		66	**Escada** Fashion F
Fashion F **Laurel**	105		65	**Bentley & Co** Jewellers
Fashion F **St John**	105-6		64	**Dixons** Cameras & electronics
Fashion F **Alexon**	107			
Fashion F **Lanvin**	108			
Sylvia Lewis Beauty Clinic	108			
Hairdressing salon **Stephen Way Hair**	109			
Shoes FM **Russell & Bromley**	109			

Brook Street | Brook Street

West side	No.	No.	East side
Barclays Bank	111	63	**FENWICK** STORE
Bond Street Silver Galleries	111		
Shoes FM **Bally**	116		
Fashion M **Cecil Gee**	120		
Lane Fine Art	123		
Arcade **Bond Street Antiques Centre**	124		
Marriage bureau **Heather Jenner**	124		
Fashion M **Herbie Frogg**	125	53	**Jasons** Fabrics
Photography **Wallace Heaton**	126	51	**The White House** Linen
Midland Bank	129	50	**Chappell Music Centre**
		49	**Bruno Magli** Shoes FM
		47	**F. Pinet** Shoes FM

Grosvenor Street | Maddox Street

West side	No.	No.	East side
Fashion F, leather goods **Loewe**	130	46	**Avi Rossini** Fashion M
Fashion M **Beale & Inman**	131	46	**Ciao** Travel
Fashion F **Beale & Inman**	133	45	**Massada** Antiques
Fabrics **Simmonds**	134	43	**Mayfair Carpet Galleries**
Fashion M **Yves Saint Laurent**	135	41	**Vittorio Arzani** Fashion M
Fashion F **Yves Saint Laurent**	137	40	**Riyahi Gallery** Fine art
		38	**Herbie on Bond Street** Fashion M

Bloomfield Place

		37	**Ermenegildo Zegna** Fashion FM
Fashion F **Marie Claire**	138	36	**Fogal** Lace
Silver & goldsmiths **S. J. Phillips**	139	34	**Sotheby's** Auctioneers
Fashion FM **Zilli**	140	30	**Herbert Johnson** Milliner FM
Antiques **Mallett**	141	29	**Gordon Scott** Shoes FM
Fashion FM **Polo Ralph Lauren**	143	28	**Celine** Accessories F
Antiques **Frank Partridge**	144	27	**Wana Designs** Fashion FM
Fine art dealers **Wildenstein**	147	26	**Tessiers** Gold & silversmiths
Fine Art Society	148	24	**Russell & Bromley** Shoes FM
Luggage **Louis Vuitton**	149		
Gifts **Isetan**	150		

Bruton Street | Conduit Street

West side	No.	No.	East side
Publishers **Time & Life**	155	23a	**Philip Landau** Fashion M
Luxury goods **Hermes**	153	23	**Moira** Antiques
Cashmeres **Ballantyne**	153a	22	**Moira** Antiques
Fashion F **Max Mara**	157	19	**Tecno** Modern furniture
Paintings **John Mitchell & Son**	160	18	**Uomo Regine** Fashion M
Fashion FM **Valentino**	160	17	Air India
Glass **Lalique**	162		
Shoes M **Churches**	163		
Employment agency **Kelly Temporary Services**	163		
Fashion FM **Savoy Tailors Guild**	164		

Clifford Street

		16	**Watches of Switzerland**

Grafton Street

West side	No.	No.	East side
		15	**Patek Phillipe** Watches
Luxury accessories **Asprey**	165	15	**George Jensen** Silversmiths
Furriers **Birger Christiansen**	170	14a	**Chopard** Luxury goods
Jewellers **Collingwood**	171	14	**Adler of Geneva** Jewellers
Jewellers **Bulgari**	172	12	**Hennell** Silversmiths
Fashion F **Karl Lagerfeld**	173	11	**Philip Antrobus** Jewellers
Gallery **Lalaounis**	174	10	**Adele Davis** Fashion F
Jewellers **Cartier**	175	10a	**Anne Bloom** Jewellers
Shoes & leatherwear **Rossetti**	177	9	**Ciro** Jewellers
Jewellers **Chaumet**	178	9	**Leger Galleries** Paintings
Fashion FM **Henry Cotton's**	179	8	**Bentley & Co** Antiques
Jewellers **Boucheron**	180	4	**Richard Green** Art gallery
Luxury goods, jewellers **Tiffany & Co**	25	1	National Westminster Bank
Fashion F **Chanel**	26		
The Royal Arcade	28		
Silver & jewellery **Holmes**	29		
Historical Portraits Ltd	30		

Burlington Gardens

Shoes FM **Bally**	30		
Shoes F **Maud Frizon**	31	24	**Salvatore Ferragamo** Shoes FM & accessories
Luxury goods **Gucci**	33	22	**Chatila** Jewellers
		20	**Pierre Cardin** Fashion FM
		19	**A. Sulka & Co** Fashion M
		18	**Alan McAfee** Shoes M

Stafford Street

West side	No.	No.	East side
		17	**Rashid** Carpets
Fashion FM **Gianni Versace**	36	17	**Clough** Jewellers & pawnbrokers
Fine art **Entwistle**	37	16	**Frost & Reed** Paintings
Antiques **Deborah Gage**	38	15	**Rayne** Shoes FM
Marlborough **Fine Art Gallery**	39	14	**Colnaghi Galleries** Paintings
Lloyds Bank	39	13	**Leger Galleries** Paintings
Employment agency **Success After Sixty**	40	13	**Benson & Hedges** Tobacconist
Fine art **Noortman**	41	10	Lufthansa German Airlines
Fine art **Thos. Agnew & Sons**	43	10	**Jindo** Fur Salon
Fine art **Thomas Gibson**	44	9	**Ginza Yamagataya** Fashion M
		7	Air Nippon Airlines
		5	**W. R. Harvey** Antiques
		4	**Fenzi** Fashion M
		3	**Belgrave Carpet Gallery**
		2	**ADC Heritage** Antique silver
		1	**F. B. Meyrowitz** Optician
		1	**Watches of Switzerland**

Green Park ⊖ | Piccadilly

South Molton Street

Oxford Street

Pub **Hog in the Pound Tavern**	28
Employment agency **Select Appointments**	28
Designer fashion F **Benetton**	23
Childrenswear **Benetton 012**	22
Bond Street Secretarial Bureau	22
Japanese jewellery **Electrum**	21
Fashion jewellery **Butler & Wilson**	20
Shoes FM **Pied à Terre**	19
Fashion F **Genny**	18
Employment agency **Reed**	17
Fashion F **Joseph**	16
Fashion F&M **Stefanel**	15
Fashion F **French for Less**	14
Designer fashion F **Arte**	12
Adventure Employment	12
Fashion F **Pied à Terre**	9
Mothers-to-be **Maman**	8
Fashion FM **Benetton**	6
Designer jewellery **André Bogaert**	5
Designer jewellery **Agatha**	4
Handbags & luggage **City Bag Store**	3
Fashion M **Daniel James**	2
Shoes FM **Benetton**	1
Restaurant **Wheelers**	1
Fashion F **Ronit Zilkha**	34

35	**Foto Inn** Developing & printing
36	**Bertie** Shoes FM
37	**Leather Rat** Leather fashion FM
39	**Browns** Fashion FM
40	**The Red Rock Cafe**
41	**The Tube** Shoes & fashion F
42	**Alma** Fashion M
43	**Saga** Japanese restaurant
43	**The Grosvenor Bureau** Employment agency
45	**Pineapple** Fashion F
45	**ROC Recruitment** Secretarial agency
46	**Widow Applebaum's** Jewish restaurant
47	**Hobbs** Designer clothes & shoes FM
48	**Grosvenor Gallery**
48	**Cable & Co** Fashion M
49	**Skindeep** Leather fashions FM
50	**Browns Labels for Less** Fashion FM
51	**Trussardi** Italian fashion FM
52	**The Vestry** Fashion FM
53	**Geno Ventti** Hairdressing salon
54	**Fabrice Karel** Fashion F
54	**Reed Accountancy** Employment agency
55	**Oliver** Fashion M
56	**Bang & Olufson** TV & hi-fi

Globe Yard

57	**Adolfo Dominguez** Hairdressing salon
57	**Molton Brown** Hairdressing salon
59	**Shane English School**
60	**London Business College**
60	**Vidal Sassoon** Hairdressing salon
63	**Pellicano** Fashion F
64	**South Molton Drug Stores**
65	**Post Office**
66	**Kenneth Jay Lane** Jewellers
67	**Monsoon** Fashion F
68	**Celia Loe** Fashion F

Regent Street

Fashion FM **Original Levi's Store**	269
Restaurant **Garfunkel's**	265
Underwear **Knickerbox**	261
Fashion F **Hennes**	260

Great Castle Street

214-216	**TOP SHOP & TOP MAN** STORE

Oxford Street

South African Airways	259
Fashion FM **Benetton**	257

266	**Shellys** Shoes FM
264	**Ratners** Jewellers
260	**Bally** Shoes FM
256	**Laura Ashley** Fashion F
254	**Thorntons** Chocolates
246	**Off the Cuff** Shirts M
	National Westminster Bank

Princes Street

Chocolates **Godiva**	247
Fashion FM **House of Scotland**	241
Cards & gifts **Clinton**	239
Cameras & film **City Photo**	239
Underwear **Damart Thermawear**	235
Fashion FM **London House**	231
Opticians **Dollond & Aitchison**	229

Little Argyll Street

244	**DICKINS & JONES** STORE

Hanover Street

Building society **Woolwich**	227
Irish airline **Aer Lingus**	223

Maddox Street

Jewellers **Pravins**	221
Telecom Electronics	219
British cloth **Court**	217
Hairdressing salon **Alan d**	215
Cyprus Government Tourist Office	213
Fashion FM, childrenswear **Scottish Wear**	209
Fashion FM **Michelle O**	207
Moroccan National Tourist Office	205
China & glass **Villeroy & Boch**	203

Great Marlborough Street

214-220	**LIBERTY** STORE
212	**Barclays Bank**
210	**The Gap** Fashion FM

Conduit Street

Bags **Henry's**	201
The Pen Shop	199
Fashion FM **The Scotch Shop**	191
Jewellery & accessories **Carré Blanc**	189
Jewellers **Peter Trevor**	189
Textiles **Court**	187
Israeli airline **El Al**	185

Foubert's Place

200	**Jaeger** Fashion FM
198	**House of Chinacraft** China & glass
188	**Hamleys** F
184	**The London House** Fabrics & woollens
170	**Mappin & Webb** Jewellers
160	**Next** Fashion FM, interiors, cafe
158	**Waterford/Wedgwood** China & glass
156	**British Airways Travellers Shop**

New Burlington Place

Noble Furs	183
Fashion FM **R.M. Williams**	181
Royal Jordanian airline **Alia**	177
Cashmeres **House of Cashmere**	175
Bureau de change	173
Saudi Arabian Airlines	171
Fashion FM **Regents**	169

Regent Street continued

<table>
<tr><td colspan="2">New Burlington Street</td><td></td><td colspan="2">Beak Street</td></tr>
<tr><td>Japanese National Tourist Organisation</td><td>167</td><td></td><td>154</td><td>Lawleys English china & glass</td></tr>
<tr><td>Fashion FM Burberrys</td><td>157</td><td></td><td>152</td><td>Bally Shoes FM</td></tr>
<tr><td>Skiwear</td><td>155</td><td></td><td>146</td><td>Viyella Shoes FM</td></tr>
<tr><td>The English Teddy Bear Company</td><td>153</td><td></td><td>144</td><td>Gap Kids Childrenswear</td></tr>
<tr><td></td><td></td><td></td><td>140</td><td>The Disney Store Gifts</td></tr>
<tr><td colspan="2">New Burlington Mews</td><td></td><td>138</td><td>The Cashmere Gallery Cashmere</td></tr>
<tr><td></td><td></td><td></td><td>134</td><td>Reject China Shop China</td></tr>
<tr><td>Fashion F The French Collection</td><td>151</td><td></td><td>132</td><td>Lloyds Bank</td></tr>
<tr><td>Fabrics The Woollens Centre</td><td>149</td><td></td><td></td><td></td></tr>
<tr><td colspan="2">Heddon Street</td><td></td><td></td><td></td></tr>
<tr><td>Singapore Airlines</td><td>145</td><td></td><td></td><td></td></tr>
<tr><td>Fashion FM Oxfords</td><td>143</td><td></td><td></td><td></td></tr>
<tr><td>Knitwear & fashions FM Scottish Woollens</td><td>141</td><td></td><td></td><td></td></tr>
<tr><td>China Rosenthal</td><td>139</td><td></td><td></td><td></td></tr>
<tr><td>China Wilson & Gill</td><td>137</td><td></td><td></td><td></td></tr>
<tr><td>Jewellers Thomas</td><td>135</td><td></td><td></td><td></td></tr>
<tr><td>Midland Bank</td><td>133</td><td></td><td></td><td></td></tr>
<tr><td colspan="2">Heddon Street</td><td></td><td colspan="2">Regent Place</td></tr>
<tr><td>Fashion FM The Highlands</td><td>129</td><td></td><td>130</td><td>Iberia Spanish airline</td></tr>
<tr><td>Fashion FM Cyril</td><td>129</td><td></td><td>126</td><td>Ryman Stationers</td></tr>
<tr><td>Fashion M Hunters</td><td>125</td><td></td><td>124</td><td>Watches of Switzerland</td></tr>
<tr><td>New Gallery Centre</td><td>123</td><td></td><td>122</td><td>Tie Rack Fashion FM</td></tr>
<tr><td>Building society Leeds Permanent</td><td>121a</td><td></td><td>114</td><td>Burton/Dorothy Perkins Fashion FM</td></tr>
<tr><td>Fabrics Fine Textiles</td><td>121</td><td></td><td>112</td><td>Garrard Gold & silversmiths</td></tr>
<tr><td>Pens Pencraft</td><td>119</td><td></td><td></td><td></td></tr>
<tr><td>Bureau de change A.M.B.</td><td>117</td><td></td><td></td><td></td></tr>
<tr><td>TSB Bank</td><td>117</td><td></td><td></td><td></td></tr>
<tr><td colspan="2">Vigo Street</td><td></td><td colspan="2">Glasshouse Street</td></tr>
<tr><td>Fashion M Austin Reed</td><td>103</td><td></td><td>100</td><td>Aquascutum Fashion FM</td></tr>
<tr><td>Shoes FM Peter Lord</td><td>101</td><td></td><td>90</td><td>Dunn & Co Fashion M</td></tr>
<tr><td>The London Textile Co</td><td>99</td><td></td><td>88</td><td>Moss Bros Fashion M</td></tr>
<tr><td>Restaurant The Veeraswamy</td><td>99</td><td></td><td>86</td><td>The Scotch House Fashion FM</td></tr>
<tr><td></td><td></td><td></td><td>82</td><td>K Shoes Shoes FM</td></tr>
<tr><td colspan="2">Swallow Street</td><td></td><td colspan="2">Quadrant Arcade</td></tr>
<tr><td>Building society Bristol & West</td><td>95</td><td></td><td>80</td><td>British Designer Knitwear Group Fashion FM</td></tr>
<tr><td>Ties, shirts M Off The Cuff</td><td>93</td><td></td><td>76</td><td>Alexandra Workwear</td></tr>
<tr><td>Handbags & luggage Salisbury</td><td>87</td><td></td><td>74a</td><td>Angus Steak House Restaurant</td></tr>
<tr><td>Bureau de change & ticket agency Eurochange</td><td>83</td><td></td><td></td><td></td></tr>
<tr><td>Gifts Chinacraft</td><td>71</td><td></td><td colspan="2">Air Street</td></tr>
<tr><td>Opticians Paris-Miki</td><td>69</td><td></td><td>70</td><td>Café Royal Restaurant & bars</td></tr>
<tr><td></td><td></td><td></td><td>62</td><td>House of Cashmeres Cashmeres</td></tr>
<tr><td colspan="2">Air Street</td><td></td><td>60</td><td>Estridge Cashmeres</td></tr>
<tr><td>Sock Shop</td><td>61</td><td></td><td>56</td><td>Stereo Regent Street Hi-fi</td></tr>
<tr><td>Fashion M Lacoste</td><td>59</td><td></td><td>52</td><td>Barclays Bank</td></tr>
<tr><td>Fashion FM Jigsaw</td><td>57</td><td></td><td></td><td></td></tr>
<tr><td>Fashion FM Tie Rack</td><td>55</td><td></td><td></td><td></td></tr>
<tr><td>Records, CDs & cassettes Tower Records</td><td>49</td><td></td><td></td><td></td></tr>
</table>

Piccadilly Circus

Kings Road

<table>
<tr><td colspan="2">Sloane Square</td><td></td><td colspan="2">Sloane Square</td></tr>
<tr><td>STORE PETER JONES</td><td></td><td></td><td></td><td>Sloane Square</td></tr>
<tr><td></td><td></td><td></td><td>9</td><td>Post Office</td></tr>
<tr><td></td><td></td><td></td><td>11</td><td>The Coffee Shop</td></tr>
<tr><td></td><td></td><td></td><td>11</td><td>HoHo Chinese restaurant</td></tr>
<tr><td></td><td></td><td></td><td>13</td><td>Next Fashion M</td></tr>
<tr><td></td><td></td><td></td><td>15</td><td>Next Fashion F</td></tr>
<tr><td></td><td></td><td></td><td>17</td><td>Forbuoys Newsagents & tobacconists</td></tr>
<tr><td></td><td></td><td></td><td>21</td><td>Ladbrokes Bookmakers</td></tr>
<tr><td></td><td></td><td></td><td>23</td><td>V. V. Rouleaux Ribbons</td></tr>
<tr><td></td><td></td><td></td><td>25</td><td>Allied-Astors Employment agency</td></tr>
<tr><td></td><td></td><td></td><td>25</td><td>Britannia Employment agency</td></tr>
<tr><td colspan="2">Cadogan Gardens</td><td></td><td>25</td><td>Lazer Fashion M</td></tr>
<tr><td>Children's wear & accessories Trotters</td><td>34</td><td></td><td>27</td><td>Eurochange Bureau de change</td></tr>
<tr><td>Children's playthings Early Learning Centre</td><td>36</td><td></td><td>29</td><td>Gadgets Gifts</td></tr>
<tr><td>Fashion F Hampstead Bazaar</td><td>38</td><td></td><td>31</td><td>Warehouse Fashion F</td></tr>
<tr><td>Fashion F Sidney Smith</td><td>36</td><td></td><td></td><td>Duke of York's Headquarters</td></tr>
<tr><td>London School of Bridge</td><td>38</td><td></td><td></td><td></td></tr>
<tr><td>Fashion M Cecil Gee</td><td>44</td><td></td><td></td><td></td></tr>
<tr><td>Wine Bar Blushes</td><td>52</td><td></td><td></td><td></td></tr>
<tr><td>Natural beauty products The Body Shop</td><td>54</td><td></td><td></td><td></td></tr>
<tr><td>Fashion FM Jeans West</td><td>54</td><td></td><td></td><td></td></tr>
<tr><td>Restaurant Pizza Hut</td><td>56</td><td></td><td></td><td></td></tr>
<tr><td>Chemist Boots</td><td>58</td><td></td><td></td><td></td></tr>
<tr><td>Shoes FM Russell & Bromley</td><td>64</td><td></td><td></td><td></td></tr>
<tr><td>Sock Shop</td><td>68</td><td></td><td></td><td></td></tr>
<tr><td colspan="2">Blacklands Terrace</td><td></td><td></td><td></td></tr>
<tr><td>Fashion FM, children's wear, home furnishings Next</td><td>72</td><td></td><td></td><td></td></tr>
</table>

Kings Road continued

West side

Lincoln Street

Restaurant **Guys & Dolls**	74
Fashion M **Next**	76
Restaurant **Pizzaland**	80
Shoes FM **The Tube**	82
Shoes FM **Hobbs**	84
Fashion F **Zoo**	86
Fashion M **Stefanel**	88
Shoes FM **Bally**	92
Fashion F **Benetton**	94
Fashion F **Warehouse**	96
Restaurant **The Chelsea Kitchen**	98
Shoes FM **Office London**	100
Fashion F **Stirling Cooper**	102

Anderson Street

Building Society **Chelsea**	112
Fashion M **Reiss**	114

Tryon Street

Fashion FM **The Leather Warehouse**	118
Shoes FM **Bertie**	118
Fashion F **Laura Ashley**	120
SHOPPING MALL KINGS WALK	
Fashion F **P.T.A.**	124
Fashion M **Woodhouse**	124a
Shoes FM **Shellys**	124b
Fashion F **Jigsaw**	124c
Fashion F **Et Vous**	126
Shoes FM **Ravel**	128
Bureau de change **Chequepoint**	130
Childrenswear **Benetton 012**	132

Bywater Street

Beauty products & comestibles **Crabtree & Evelyn**	134
Fashion FM **Legacy**	136
Building society **Abbey National**	138
Ice-cream **Haagen-Dazs**	138a

Markham Square

Books **Book Bargains**	140
Art gallery **Dryden Gallery**	144
Greetings cards **Post Impressions**	146

Markham Street

Chemist **Boots**	150
Restaurant **The Pheasantry**	152
Stationery **Ryman**	152
Books **Dillons**	152

Jubilee Place

Lloyds Bank	164
Fashion FM **Chelsea Leather**	168
Film processing **Snappy Snaps**	170
Restaurant **Choy's**	172
Shoes FM **Blue Velvet**	174
Opticians **Chelsea Eye Centre**	176

Burnsall Street

Fashion M **4 You Tailoring Company**	178
Shoes FM **R. Soles**	178a
Fashion M **Forest Ranger**	182
New age gifts **Paradise Farm**	182a
Teas & coffees **Whittard**	184
Fashion FM **Soldier Blue**	184a

East side

Cheltenham Terrace

33	National Westminster Bank
33a	**Blazer** Fashion M
33b	**Queue** Fashion FM
33c	**Chipie** Fashion M
33d	**Monsoon** Fashion F
33e	**Martins of Chelsea** TV & hi-fi
33f	**Eyetech** Opticians
33g	**Pied à Terre** Shoes FM
33h	**Our Price** Records, CDs & cassettes

Walpole Street

35	**Safeway** Supermarket

Royal Avenue

49	**McDonald's** Restaurant
51	**William Hill** Bookmakers
53	**Pineapple** Fashion F
55	**Arte** Fashion F
57	**Helen Storey** Fashion F
59	**Karen Millen** Fashion F

Wellington Street

61	**Dentics** Dentist
63	**Vanilla** Hair & beauty
65	**Sonico Jeans** Fashion M
67a	**Harvest** Leather fashion M
69	**Review** Fashion M

Smith Street

69a	**Sissors** Hairdressing salon
71	**Morgan** Fashion F
73	**Bruce Jeremy** Fashion F
75	**In Wear** Fashion FM
79	**New Man** Fashion M
85	**Marks & Spencer** Foods
97	**Cotton Club** Fashion F
99	**Woodhouse** Fashion M
	Car Park
105	**Heaven** Fashion FM
107	**Gallery** Restaurant
109a	**R. Soles** Leather boots
109	**The Poster Shop**
113	**Rivaaz** Leatherwear FM
115	**Kodo** Fashion F

Radnor Walk

119	**Chelsea Potter** Pub & restaurant
121	**The Common Market** Fashion FM
123	**Victoria Wine** Wine merchants
123a	**Awards** Fashion FM

Shawfield Street

125	**Full Power** Fashion F
127	**Picasso** Restaurant
129	**Slot Machine** Fashion M
131	**Hyper Hyper** Fashion F
135	**Quincy** Fashion M
137	**Antiquarius** Antiques, fashion FM
139	**Basia Zarsycka** Bridalwear, shoes, jewellery
141	**Edwina Ronay** Fashion F

Kings Road continued

		Flood Street
Dry cleaners **Sketchley**	186	
Leather fashion FM **Sloane's Leathers**	186a	
Fashion FM **Leather Technics**	188a	
Candles **Angelic**	196	
Supermarket **Waitrose**	198	
Pub **The Trafalgar**	200	
Chelsea Cinema	206	
Furnishings **Habitat**	206	
	145	**Jaeger** Fashion FM
	147	**Quarzo** Fashion FM
	150	**Omcar** Fashion FM
	153	**Boy** Fashion M
	155	**Original Levi's Store** Fashion FM
	155a	Chelsea Methodist Church
	157	**Hittite** Fashion F
	159	**Leather Machine** Leather fashion FM, records
	161	**The Boot Store** Shoes M

Chelsea Manor Street — **Chelsea Manor Street**

National Westminster Bank	224	
Post Office	232	
Household goods **Reject Shop**	234	
		TOWN HALL
		Citizen's Advice Bureau
	181	**Chenil Galleries**
	185	**David Clulow** Opticians
	187	**Photo-Optix** Cameras

Sydney Street

	191	**Phlip** Fashion FM
	195	**Henry J Bean's Bar & Grill** Bar
COUNCIL OFFICES	250	
	199	**Video Shuttle** Videos
	201	**Amagansett** Fashion M
	203	**Chelsea Audio-Visual Centre**
	205	**Pucci Pizza** Italian restaurant

Dovehouse Street

| | 207 | **Givans** Linen |
| | 209 | **Oddbins** Wine merchants |

CHELSEA FIRE STATION

Manresa Road — **Oakley Street**

KING'S COLLEGE LONDON

Glebe Place

	221	**My Old Dutch** Restaurant
	229	**Naf-Naf** Fashion FM, childrenswear
	235	**Café Tempo** Restaurant
	237	**Chelsea Food Fayre**

Bramerton Street

Carlyle Square

	241	**Designers Sale Studio** Fashion F
	245a	**Antique Market**
	247	**Joanna Booth** Antiques
	249	**Made In Italy** Restaurant
	251	**S. Borris** Delicatessen
	253	**Chelsea Antique Market**
	255	**Isaac. T. Lloyd** Chemist
	257	**Newsagents**
	259	**Green & Stone** Artists' materials
	269	**David Pettifer** Antiques
	271	**Designers Guild** Furnishings
	271b	**The Stockpot** Restaurant
Estate agents **De Groot Collis**	296	275 **David Tron** Antiques
Pub **Cadogan Arms**	298	277 **Designers Guild** Fabric & wallpapers

Church Street — **Old Church Street**

National Westminster Bank	300	279 MGM Cinema
Interior designers **Osborne & Little**	304	279 **Mr Light** Lighting
Antiques **Godson & Coles**	310	279 **Europa Foods** Supermarket
Restaurant **Le Gourmet**	312	279c **Delcor** Interiors
Artists' materials **Chelsea Art Stores**	314	281 **Brats** Gifts & cards
Restaurant **The Argyle**	316	283 **Wilde One's** Ethnic fashion & gifts
Maps & prints **Old Church Galleries**	320	285 **Megalomania** Fashion FM
Furniture **Sofa Workshop**	324	287 **Raffles** Club
Carpets **Bernadout**	328	289 **Sasha Hetherington** Evening wear F
Restaurant **Lo Spuntino**	330	289a **The Jam** Restaurant
Restaurant **Big Easy**	334	289 **Joanna's Tent** Fashion FM & childrenswear
Antiques **Monro Heywood**	336	
Furniture **William Yeoward**	336	
Restaurant **Travellers**	338	**Paultons Square**
Restaurant **Thierry's**	342	
Antiques **Tony Buzzi**	344	303 **Hooper & Purchase** Antiques
Barclays Bank	348	305 **Bamboo Kitchen** Chinese take-away
		307 **Kriston** Hand-finished launderers

The Vale

		309 **Million Dollar Sports** Sportswear
		313 **Chelsea Rare Books**
Fashion M **Nigel Hall**	350	317 **Gregor Schumi** Hairdressing salon
Designer fashion FM, hairdresser, bar **The Garage**	350	319 **J. & F. E. Simpson** Jewellers
Wellworth Food & Wines	350	321 **Rococo** Chocolates
Fashion M **Daniel James**	352	323 **Dept.** Shoes & fashion M
National Westminster Bank	352a	

Beaufort Street

EATING & DRINKING

Restaurants

These have been chosen for authentic food and good cooking. For more detailed information on where and what to eat see Nicholson's London Restaurant Guide.
Restaurant Services (081-888 8080) and Direct Dining (071-287 3287) offer free up-to-the-minute information and advice on London's restaurants and can make table reservations.

The following price guide refers to a three-course meal for one including VAT but without wine:

£ - £10.00 and under
££ - £10.00-£20.00
£££ - £20.00-£30.00
£££+ - £30.00 and over

(Reserve) - advisable to reserve
Open to . . . - last orders

A - Access/Mastercard/Eurocard
Ax - American Express
Dc - Diners Club
V - Visa/Barclaycard

B - Breakfast
L - Lunch
D - Dinner

Service charge: *many restaurants add service on to the bill, usually at 12½%, but do not always say so – if in doubt, ask. However, they do usually say if service is not included.*

AFRICAN & CARIBBEAN
Afric-Carib
1 Stroud Green Rd N4. 071-263 7440. Restaurant and take-away specialising in spicy Nigerian dishes. Chicken, beef or fish with plantains and yams. Relaxed, informal atmosphere. *LD open to 23.30.* A.V. **£**

Brixtonian Backyard   **4 F2**
4 Neal's Yard, off Neal St WC2. 071-240 2769. Large, bright restaurant with West Indian menu. Deep fried salt cod, chicken Columbo, sweet potato and salmon patties. *LD open to 23.30. Closed Sun & Mon.* A.V. **££**

AMERICAN
Criterion Brasserie   **4 E3**
Piccadilly Circus W1. 071-925 0909. Housed in a Victorian entertainment complex. Cuisine is Cal-Ital; dishes include veal parmesan sandwich, Caesar salad and fried spaghetti. *LD open to 23.30*. A.Ax.Dc.V. **££**

Hard Rock Café   **4 C5**
150 Old Park Lane W1. 071-629 0382. Ever popular hamburger joint, just off Hyde Park Corner. Vast room on two levels with good quality food and non-stop rock. Occasional queues outside. *LD open to 24.00*. Ax.V. **££**

Joe Allen   **4 F3**
13 Exeter St WC2. 071-836 0651. In a converted Covent Garden warehouse, this London branch follows the pattern of its New York and Paris counterparts. Cocktail bar and blackboard menu of steaks, hamburgers, ribs and chilli followed by cheesecake or brownies. Fashionably crowded, especially after the theatre. *LD (Reserve) open to 00.45, to 24.00 Sun*. No credit cards. **££**

Smollensky's Balloon   **4 D4**
1 Dover St W1. 071-491 1199. Big, light and bustling restaurant and bar on two floors. Generous portions – speciality is steaks, with a choice of seven sauces. Rich desserts – chocolate mousse, peanut butter cheesecake. *LD open to 24.00, to 22.30 Sun*. A.Ax.Dc.V. **££**

BELGIAN
Belgo   **1 D1**
72 Chalk Farm Rd NW1. 071-267 0718. Jolly, entertaining restaurant which you enter through a tunnel and where the waiters wear habits. Moules au gratin, wild boar sausages with stoemp. Belgian beers. *LD open to 23.30*. A.Ax.V. **££**

CENTRAL EUROPEAN
Kerzenstüberl   **4 B2**
9 St Christopher's Place W1. 071-486 3196. Authentic Austrian dishes accompanied by accordion music, dancing and singing. *LD (Reserve) open to 23.00. Licensed to 01.00. Closed Sat L & Sun*. A.Ax.Dc.V. **££**

Old Vienna Budapest   **4 C3**
94 New Bond St W1. 071-629 8716. Lavishly decorated, traditional Austrian restaurant. Specialities from Austria and Hungary – expect to be serenaded at your table by the resident singer! *LD open to 01.00, to 22.30 Sun*. A.Ax.Dc.V. **££**

St Moritz   **4 E3**
161 Wardour St W1. 071-734 3324. Two floors rigged out like a ski hut in the famous Swiss resort. Cheese and beef

fondues are the house speciality. *LD (Reserve) open to 23.30. Closed Sat L & Sun*. A.Ax.Dc.V. **££**

CHINESE
Dragon Gate   4 E3
7 Gerrard St W1. 071-734 5154. The first and probably best Szechuan restaurant in London. Sliced pork with garlic and chilli, tea-smoked duck. Pancakes or almond curd to follow. *LD open to 23.30*. A.Ax.Dc.V. **££**

Ken Lo's Memories of China   7 A2
67-69 Ebury St SW1. 071-730 7734. The windows are etched with Tang dynasty horses and the menu features regional specialities: Shanghai sea bass, Szechuan crispy beef, Cantonese seafood with black bean sauce. *LD open to 23.00. Closed Sun*. A.Ax.Dc.V. **£££+**

Lee Ho Fook   4 E3
15-16 Gerrard St W1. 071-734 9578. Renowned Cantonese cooking, very popular with the local Chinese. Huge portions at reasonable prices. Dim sum at *lunchtime. LD open to 23.30, to 22.30 Sun*. A.Ax.Dc.V. **££**

Poons   4 E3
4 Leicester Sq WC2. 071-437 1528. Wind-dried meats are a speciality at this family-run Cantonese restaurant. Unlicensed branch at 27 Lisle St WC2 (**4 E3**). 071-437 4549. *LD (Reserve) open to 23.30. Closed Sun*. No credit cards. **££**

EAST EUROPEAN
Borshtch 'n' Tears   3 G6
46 Beauchamp Place SW3. 071-589 5003. Crowded, informal and lively Russian restaurant. Borshtch, beef Stroganoff, chicken Dragomiroff and blinis served to the accompaniment of Russian music. *D open to 01.15, to 00.15 Sun*. Ax. **££**

Daquise   6 D2
20 Thurloe St SW7. 071-589 6117. Polish restaurant popular with Polish émigrés. Serves traditional, simple and inexpensive dishes: borshtch, bigor and sausages. Also afternoon tea with excellent pastries. *LD open to 23.30*. No credit cards. **£**

Gay Hussar   4 E2
2 Greek St W1. 071-437 0973. Intimate, cosy, much-loved Hungarian restaurant. Try the stuffed cabbage, chilled wild cherry soup, pike with beetroot sauce. *LD (Reserve) open to 23.00. Closed Sun*. Ax. **££**

Luba's Bistro   3 F6
6 Yeoman's Row SW3. 071-589 '2950. Authentic Russian cooking. Sit at long tables and bring your own wine. Beef Stroganoff, kooliebaiaka (salmon pie), zrazra (chicken with vegetables). *D open to 24.00. Closed Sun*. A.V. **££**

ENGLISH
English House   6 F2
3 Milner St SW3. 071-584 3002. Intimate restaurant in the
style of an English country house. Classic English cooking. *LD
(Reserve) open to 23.30, to 22.00 Sun.* A.Ax.Dc.V. **£££+**

Porters   4 F3
17 Henrietta St WC2. 071-836 6466. Large, pillared dining
room lined with old carvings and mirrors. Imaginative, good
value English fare in the form of pies – Billingsgate, lamb and
apricot, turkey and chestnut. Bread and butter pudding,
rhubarb crumble or Stilton to follow. Also traditional Sunday
lunch. *LD open to 23.30.* A.V. **££**

Rules   4 F3
35 Maiden Lane WC2. 071-836 5314. Something of a
landmark, rich in associations – Dickens, Thackeray,
Edward VII and Lillie Langtry all dined here. Jugged hare,
steak and kidney pie, grouse and venison. Booking
essential. *LD (Reserve) open to 24.00. Closed Sun.*
A.Ax.Dc.V. **£££**

Simpson's-in-the-Strand   4 F3
100 Strand WC2. 071-836 9112. An English institution with an
Edwardian club atmosphere. Excellent fish and meat dishes –
smoked salmon, Dover sole, duck or saddle of mutton. Fine
wines and vintage port. Booking and correct dress essential.
LD (Reserve) open to 23.00. Closed Sun. A.Ax.Dc.V. **£££**

Tiddy Dols   4 C4
55 Shepherd Market W1. 071-499 2357. Unique, comfortable
restaurant spreading over several houses dating from 1741.
Low ceilings and winding staircases abound. Fillet of venison,
beef Wellington, cock-a-leekie and the original gingerbread
Tiddy Dol on the menu. Live entertainment. *D (Reserve) open
to 23.30.* A.Ax.V. **£££**

FISH
Bentley's   4 D3
11-15 Swallow St W1. 071-734 4756. Famous seafood
restaurant and oyster bar. Wide variety of fish, plus excellent
oysters, prawns and crab. *LD (Reserve) open to 22.45. Closed
Sun.* A.Ax.Dc.V. **£££+**

Overton's   7 B1
4-6 Victoria Bldgs, Terminus Place SW1. 071-834 3774. Also at
5 St James's St SW1 (**4 D4**). 071-839 3744. Long-established
fish restaurant with an olde-worlde atmosphere. Oysters,
lobster, Dover sole. *LD (Reserve) open to 22.30. Closed Sun.*
A.Ax.Dc.V. **£££**

Sheekey's   4 F3
28 St Martin's Court WC2. 071-240 2565. One of London's

oldest fish restaurants. Excellent oysters, lobster and turbot. *LD open to 23.15. Closed Sun.* A.Ax.Dc.V. **£££**

Sweetings   **5 D3**
39 Queen Victoria St EC4. 071-248 3062. Tiny 150-year-old City eatery. Excellent service and very popular so queueing often necessary. *L open to 15.00. Closed Sat & Sun.* No credit cards. **££**

Wheeler's Old Compton Street   **4 E2**
19 Old Compton St W1. 071-437 2706. Popular chain of restaurants specialising in expertly cooked fish dishes. Welcoming yet sophisticated atmosphere. Scallops, lobster Normande, sole Egyptian and shellfish. Several other branches. *LD (Reserve) open to 23.00.* A.Ax.Dc.V. **£££**

FRENCH

Ark   **3 C4**
122 Palace Gdns Terrace W8. 071-229 4024. Also at 35 Kensington High St W8 (**3 B6**). 071-937 4294. Cosy and friendly atmosphere with good French provincial food. Onion soup, noisette d'agneau, foie de veau. *LD (Reserve) open to 23.15. Closed Sun L.* A.Ax.V. **££**

Boulestin   **4 F3**
1a Henrietta St WC2. 071-836 7061. Famous old restaurant opened in the 1920s. Club-like atmosphere with a menu offering sumptuous dishes such as crabe à l'artichaut, ballotine de turbot farcie au homard, tulipe de sorbets. Fine wines, dignified service. *LD open to 23.15. Closed Sat L & Sun.* A.Ax.Dc.V. **£££+**

Claridges Restaurant   **4 C3**
Brook St W1. 071-629 8860. Distinguished French cooking in luxurious surroundings. The atmosphere is typical of the sedate thirties. Polished service and a notable wine list. *LD (Reserve) open to 24.00.* A.Ax.Dc.V. **£££+**

L'Epicure   **4 E2**
28 Frith St W1. 071-437 2829. Confident, flamboyant establishment with excellent French cuisine. Speciality is flambés, also steak maison, crêpes suzette and kidneys in marsala. *LD (Reserve) open to 23.15. Closed Sat L & Sun.* A.Ax.Dc.V. **£££**

L'Escargot   **4 E2**
48 Greek St W1. 071-437 6828. A Soho institution. Brasserie on the ground floor offers reasonably priced and varied dishes; upstairs the French restaurant is more formal. Menu changes every two months. Excellent wine list. *LD (Reserve) open to 23.15. Closed Sat L & Sun.* A.Ax.Dc.V. **£££**

Le Gavroche   **4 B3**
43 Upper Brook St W1. 071-408 0881. One of the best restaurants in London, renowned for its luxurious atmosphere and

imaginative *haute cuisine*. Cooking and service faultless. *LD (Reserve) open to 23.00. Closed Sat & Sun.* A.Ax.Dc.V. **£££**+

Langan's Brasserie 4 C4

Stratton St W1. 071-493 6437. Vast room with a carefully contrived atmosphere of decaying splendour. One of London's most fashionable eating places (co-owned by Michael Caine). Excellent classic French cuisine from a small menu. *LD (Reserve) open to 23.00, to 24.00 Sat. Closed Sat L & Sun.* A.Ax.Dc.V. **£££**+

Mon Plaisir 4 F2

21 Monmouth St WC2. 071-836 7243. Small, typically French restaurant. Short, unpretentious menu; escalope à la crème, coq au vin. Friendly atmosphere and helpful service. *LD (Reserve) open to 23.15. Closed Sat L & Sun.* A.Ax.Dc.V. **££**

GREEK, TURKISH & CYPRIOT

Beotys 4 F3

79 St Martin's Lane WC2. 071-836 8768. Comfortable establishment with authentic Greek cooking. Stuffed vine leaves, kalamarakia (squid cooked in its own ink), moussaka, baklava and kadeifi. Cypriot wines. *LD open to 23.30. Closed Sun.* A.Ax.Dc.V. **££**

Divan 3 F1

228 Edgware Rd W2. 071-724 7257. Bright and welcoming Turkish restaurant with appetising national dishes. *LD open to 24.00, to 23.00 Sun.* A.Ax.Dc.V. **££**

Lemonia 1 B1

89 Regent's Park Rd NW1. 071-586 7454. Mediterranean atmosphere in this busy Greek restaurant. Wonderful meze, lamb souvlaki and fish shashlik. *LD open to 23.30. Closed Sat L & Sun D.* No credit cards. **££**

Mega Kalamaras 3 C3

76 Inverness Mews W2. 071-727 9122. Also smaller and less expensive **Mikro Kalamaras** 66 Inverness Mews W2. 071-727 9122. True taverna atmosphere. Superb national dishes ranging from dolmades to baklava. Bouzouki players on some evenings and dancing. *D (Reserve) open to 24.00* (Mikro *to 23.30). Closed Sun.* A.Ax.Dc.V. **££**

White Tower 4 E1

1 Percy St W1. 071-636 8141. Elegant, first class cuisine in London's first Greek restaurant. Lengthy menu and refined atmosphere; moussaka, shashlik and duck with bulghur. *LD (Reserve) open to 22.30. Closed Sat & Sun.* A.Ax.Dc.V. **£££**

INDIAN

Bombay Brasserie 6 C2

Bailey's Hotel, 140 Gloucester Rd SW7. 071-370 4040. Large, fashionable restaurant decorated in colonial style.

Representative dishes from several regions including Bombay thali, Goan fish curry. *LD (Reserve D) open to 24.00.* A.Dc.V. L **££** D **£££**

Khan's   3 C2
13-15 Westbourne Grove W1. 071-727 5420. Vast room with oriental arches and palm tree pillars. Cheap, cheerful and noisy with excellent north Indian cuisine. *LD (Reserve D) open to 24.00.* A.Ax.Dc.V. **£**

Last Days of the Raj   4 F2
22 Drury Lane WC2. 071-836 1628. Bengali specialities in crowded theatreland restaurant. Meat thali, lamb tandoori, hot and sour chicken. *LD (Reserve) open to 23.30. Closed Sun L.* A.Ax.Dc.V. **££**

Red Fort   4 E2
77 Dean St W1. 071-437 2115. Widely regarded as one of the best Indian restaurants in London. Warm pink decor, tropical greenery and soft lighting create a palatial atmosphere in which to try Moghul Indian dishes. Quails in mild spice, chicken korahi, tandooris and nan breads. Cocktail bar. *LD (Reserve) open to 23.30, to 23.00 Sun.* A.Ax.Dc.V. **££**

Veeraswamy   4 D3
99-101 Regent St (entrance in Swallow St) W1. 071-734 1401. Excellent, authentic food in atmosphere of a pre-war Indian club. Traditionally dressed waiters, and a large choice of curries – Moglai, Delhi, Madras, Ceylon and Vindaloo. *LD (Reserve) open to 23.15, to 22.00 Sun.* A.Ax.Dc.V. **££**

INEXPENSIVE EATING
The following are places where you can eat a good meal for **£10.00 or under**. The café serving 'sausage, egg and chips' is not included here, neither are the fast food chains which can be found on nearly every high street. This list features restaurants with distinctive or unusual cooking and atmosphere – but particularly those that are good value for money.

Bistro Vino   6 D2
1 Old Brompton Rd SW7. 071-589 3888. Also at 5 Clareville St SW7 (**6 C2**). 071-373 3903. Separately managed but similar style informal restaurants. Good simple bistro food at very reasonable prices in cheerful, lively surroundings. *LD open to 23.30.* (Clareville St *D only*). A.V. **£**

Chelsea Kitchen   6 E3
98 King's Rd SW3. 071-589 1330. The daily menu offers a good choice of hot, cheap dishes. Soup, moussaka, spaghetti. Licensed. *LD open to 23.45.* No credit cards. **£**

Ed's Easy Diner   4 E2
12 Moor St (off Old Compton St) W1. 071-439 1955. Also at 362 King's Rd SW3 (**6 B6**). 071-352 1956. American-style diner

with counter-top jukeboxes and bar seating. Hamburgers and fries dominate, but also club sandwiches and salads. US imported beers, thick milkshakes and malts. *LD open to 24.00, to 01.00 Fri & Sat.* No credit cards. **£**

Geales
3 B4

2-4 Farmer St W8. 071-727 7969. Large selection of excellent fish and chips. Cod's roe, clams, sole. Licensed. *LD open to 23.00. Closed Sun & Mon.* A.V. **£**

The Lantern

23a Malvern Rd NW6. 071-624 1796. Amazing variety and quality at low prices. French bistro with simple, candlelit ambience, soft music, blackboard menu and wine list. Predictably busy. *LD (Reserve Fri & Sat) open to 24.00, to 23.00 Sun.* A.V. **£**

My Old Dutch
4 G1

131 High Holborn WC1. 071-242 5200. Traditional Dutch farmhouse decor, pine tables and chairs. Over 100 generous sized savoury and sweet pancakes. *LD open to 23.45.* A.Ax.Dc.V. **£**

Pizza Express
1 G6

30 Coptic St WC1. 071-636 2244. Modern pizza parlour with a large oven in the middle, so you can see your pizza being cooked. Many varieties. Numerous branches. Live jazz at 10 Dean St W1 (**4 E2**). 071-437 9595. *LD open to 24.00.* A.Ax.V. **£**

Spaghetti House
4 E3

24 Cranbourn St WC2. 071-836 8168. Genuine Italian spaghetti house, friendly and busy. Soups, pasta dishes, pastries and ice-cream. Several branches. Disco at Vecchia Milano, 74-77 Welbeck St W1 (**4 C2**). 071-935 2371. *LD open to 23.00. Closed Sun.* A.Ax.Dc.V. **£**

Standard
3 C2

23 Westbourne Grove W2. 071-727 4818. Large, popular Indian restaurant serving over 80 specialities including tandoori and vegetarian dishes. *LD (Reserve) open to 24.00.* A.Ax.Dc.V. **£**

Stockpot
4 E3

40 Panton St SW1. 071-839 5142. Also at 6 Basil St SW3 (**3 G5**). 071-589 8627. Crowded, noisy and excellent value. Home-made soups, casseroles and puddings. *LD open to 23.00, to 22.00 Sun* (Basil St *closed Sun*). No credit cards. **£**

Wong Kei
4 E3

41-43 Wardour St W1. 071-437 8408. Large, cheap and cheerful Cantonese restaurant on four floors. Always busy and bustling; expect to share a table! *LD open to 23.15.* No credit cards or cheques. **£**

INTERNATIONAL
Neal Street Restaurant
4 F2

26 Neal St WC2. 071-836 8368. Chic and modern with elegantly prepared dishes culled from international recipes.

Prawns wrapped in bacon, scrambled egg with smoked eel, roast duck with apple sauce. *LD (Reserve) open to 23.00. Closed Sat & Sun.* A.Ax.Dc.V. **£££**

Phood 4 D2

31 Foubert's Place W1. 071-494 4192. An eclectic menu which includes Thai fishcakes, eggs Benedict, several vegetarian choices, plus steak sandwiches and salads on the snack menu. *LD open to 23.00. Closed Sun.* A.Ax.V. A la carte **£££** snack menu **£**

Pomegranates 7 C4

94 Grosvenor Rd SW1. 071-828 6560. Highly original and adventurous restaurant. Good value, set price menu is an amalgam of international dishes including Creole, West Indian, Chinese, French and Italian influences. Multi-national wine list. *LD (Reserve D) open to 23.15. Closed Sat L & Sun.* A.Ax.Dc.V. L **££** D **£££**

ITALIAN

Biagi's 3 G2

39 Upper Berkeley St W1. 071-723 0394. Well-run, intimate trattoria decorated with fishing nets. Good varied Italian dishes. Scallopine alla crema, entrecôte alla pizzaiola, saltimbocca. *LD (Reserve) open to 23.00.* A.Ax.Dc.V. **££**

Kettners 4 E3

29 Romilly St W1. 071-437 6437. There has been a restaurant here since the mid-19thC. Sumptuous interior, probably the most pleasant setting for pizzas and hamburgers (owned by the Pizza Express chain). Champagne bar. Pianist *every evening. LD (no reservations) open to 24.00.* A.Ax.Dc.V. **££**

Leoni's Quo Vadis 4 E2

26-29 Dean St W1. 071-437 4809. One of Soho's oldest and most famous restaurants, in the same building where Karl Marx once lived. Excellent traditional cuisine; fettucine Quo Vadis, with cream, tomato and fresh basil, is one of the favourites. *LD (Reserve) open to 23.15, to 22.30 Sun.* A.Ax.Dc.V. **£££**

Luigi's 4 F3

15 Tavistock St WC2. 071-240 1795. Something of an institution, often crowded and popular with after-theatre diners. Photographs of entertainment personalities decorate the walls. Good, authentic food: cannelloni, grilled mussels, veal and chicken dishes. *LD (Reserve) open to 23.30. Closed Sun.* A.Dc.V. **£££**

San Lorenzo 3 G6

22 Beauchamp Place SW3. 071-584 1074. One of London's best known Italian restaurants offering excellent traditional cuisine. Fashionable clientele enjoy the unusual veal and chicken dishes. Extensive wine list. Outdoor seating in summer. *LD (Reserve) open to 23.30. Closed Sun.* No credit cards. **£££**

JAPANESE
Masako   4 B2
6-8 St Christopher's Place W1. 071-935 1579. Authentic Japanese restaurant with private dining rooms attended by charming waitresses in kimonos. Wide-ranging menu including set sukiyaki and tempura meals. *LD open to 22.00. Closed Sun.* A.Ax.Dc.V. **£££**+

Wagamama   4 F1
4 Streatham St, off Bloomsbury St WC1. 071-323 9223. Noodle bar with sleek decor. Huge bowls of ramen noodle soup and fried rice or noodles with vegetables or seafood toppings. All served by super-efficient waiters and waitresses wielding hand-held computer pads. Non-smoking. *LD open to 23.00. Closed Sun.* No credit cards. **£**

JEWISH
Bloom's   5 G2
90 Whitechapel High St E1. 071-247 6001. Also at 130 Golders Green Rd NW11. 081-455 1338. Bustling kosher restaurants, offering large helpings of gefilte fisch, lockshen pudding, meatballs, salt beef, stuffed kishka. *LD open to 21.30. Closed Fri D, Sat & Jewish hols.* A.Ax.V. **££**

Widow Applebaum's   4 C3
46 South Molton St W1. 071-629 4649. American-Jewish deli offering 101 dishes. Mirrors and photos of New York in the jazz age and wooden benches outside for *summer* eating. Matzo balls, hot salt beef and pastrami, apfelstrüdel and ice-cream sodas. *LD open to 19.30. Closed Sat D & Sun.* No credit cards. **£**

KOREAN
Arirang   4 D2
31-32 Poland St W1. 071-437 9662. Green and white decor, lacquered vases and a bamboo ceiling. Waitresses in Korean dress steer you through the large menu which may include kim chee (hot pickled cabbage), yuk kwe (beef strips with pear). Sake and ginseng to drink. *LD (Reserve) open to 23.00. Closed Sun.* A.Ax.Dc.V. **£££**

Shilla   4 D2
58-69 Great Marlborough St W1. 071-434 1650. Charming service to help you with the speciality here – barbecue dishes. Delicious sauces accompany beef, chicken or seafood. Set menus available. *LD open to 22.30.* A.Ax.Dc.V. **££**

MEXICAN
La Cucaracha   4 E2
12-13 Greek St W1. 071-734 2253. London's first Mexican restaurant, in the cellars of a converted monastery. Hacienda-

style decor with a sunny covered terrace at the back. Ceviche, tacos, burritos, enchiladas. *LD open to 23.30. Closed Sun.* A.Ax.Dc.V. **££**

Los Locos 4 F3
24 Russell St WC2. 071-379 0220. Also at 14 Soho St W1 (**4 E2**). 071-287 0005. Mexican bar and restaurant with lots of Tex-Mex specials. Nachos, tacos, carnitas, steaks, enchiladas, fajitas cooked over mesquite wood. Mexican beers and cocktails. *Disco from 23.30 every night. D open to 03.00.* A.Ax.Dc.V. **££**

MODERN EUROPEAN
Alastair Little 4 E2
49 Frith St W1. 071-734 5183. Fashionable restaurant with an imaginative, frequently changing menu. Tempting, delicious results such as tomato and basil soup, noisettes of lamb with exotic fungi. *LD (Reserve) open to 23.00. Closed Sat L & Sun.* A.V. **£££**

Bibendum 6 E2
81 Fulham Rd SW3. 071-581 5817. Delightful restaurant within the unusual 1910 Michelin building. Simple, elegant and inventive French and English dishes. Carefully chosen wine list. *LD (Reserve) open to 23.00, to 22.30 Sun.* A.V. **£££+**

Chanterelle 6 C3
119 Old Brompton Rd SW3. 071-373 5522. Attractive, atmospheric decor in this popular, busy restaurant. Good value set menus may include mousse of Stilton and Armagnac, trout marinated in white wine. *LD (Reserve) open to 23.30.* A.Ax.Dc.V. *L* **£** *D* **££**

Odin's 1 D6
27 Devonshire St W1. 071-935 7296. Stylish, luxurious and decorated with interesting photographs, prints and paintings. Frequently changing à la carte menu may include red mullet pâté, stuffed roast duck, rack of lamb. *LD (Reserve) open to 23.15. Closed Sat & Sun.* Ax.V. **£££**

OPEN-AIR EATING
Barbican, Waterside Café 2 E6
Level 5, Barbican Centre EC2. 071-638 4141. Modern self-service café by the man-made lake of the arts centre. Snacks or full meals. *LD open to 20.00.* No credit cards. **£-££**

Dan's 6 E3
119 Sydney St SW3. 071-352 2718. Bright, airy room with hanging plants and seating in a rear garden. English and French cuisine. Try the warm spinach mousse with basil coulis, rack of lamb with honey and mustard. *LD open to 22.30. Closed Sat L.* A.Ax.Dc.V. *L* **££** *D* **£££**

La Famiglia   **6 C4**
7 Langton St SW10. 071-351 0761. Attractive, with pretty rear
garden and southern Italian cooking. Fourteen types of pasta
available. Italian wines. *LD open to 23.30.* A.Ax.Dc.V. **£££+**

SCANDINAVIAN
Anna's Place
90 Mildmay Park N1. 071-249 9379. Small, intimate restaurant
in Anna's home serving excellent Scandinavian and French
food. Camembert with parsley, gravadlax, beef or herring,
duck breast with Swedish cabbage. *LD (Reserve) open to
22.45. Closed Sun & Mon.* No credit cards. **££**

Garbo's   **1 B6**
42 Crawford St W1. 071-262 6582. Pleasant pink restaurant
serving Scandinavian home cooking. Herring salad Baltic,
cabbage stuffed with minced pork, beef and rice or smoked
eel. Imported Swedish beers and Schnapps. *LD (Reserve)
open to 23.30. Closed Sat L & Sun L.* A.Ax.V. **££**

SOUTH EAST ASIAN
Desaru   **4 E3**
60-62 Old Compton St W1. 071-734 4379. A very busy
Indonesian/Malaysian restaurant, convenient for the theatre.
Choice of set menus to help those in a hurry. Good noodle
dishes and specialities. *LD open to 23.45, to 22.00 Sun.*
A.Ax.V. **££**

Lemongrass   **1 E1**
243 Royal College St NW1. 071-284 1116. An eclectic restaurant serving Vietnamese, Thai, Cambodian and Chinese dishes. *LD open to 22.45. Closed Sat L & Sun L.* A.V. **££**

Rasa Sayang   **4 E2**
10 Frith St W1. 071-734 8720. Unpretentious restaurant offering authentic Singaporean, Indonesian and Malaysian food. Try
the beef satay, prawns, gado gado. *LD (Reserve D) open to
23.30. Closed Sat L.* A.Ax.Dc.V. **££**

SPANISH & PORTUGUESE
Caravela   **3 F6**
39 Beauchamp Place SW3. 071-581 2366. Small, intimate
basement Portuguese restaurant. The menu is largely
seafood, with fresh grilled sardines, prawns piri piri and regional specialities. Wine list exclusively Portuguese. Live music in
the *evening. LD (Reserve) open to 01.00, to 24.00 Sun. Closed
Sun L.* A.Ax.Dc.V. **££**

Valencia   **6 A4**
1 Empress Approach, Lillie Rd SW6. 071-385 0039. London's
oldest Spanish restaurant. Large menu of regional dishes and

wine list strong on Rioja and Catalan wines. Guitarist *every night. D open to 00.15.* A.V. **££**

THAI

Bahn Thai   4 E2
21a Frith St W1. 071-437 8504. Stylish decor and high-quality authentic Thai food make this a popular restaurant where the dishes are chilli-rated for spiciness! Unusual dishes such as silver pomfret in chilli. Vegetarians well catered for. Fiery Thai whisky to drink. *LD (Reserve) open to 23.15.* A.Ax.V. **££**

Blue Elephant   6 A5
4-5 Fulham Broadway SW6. 071-385 6595. One of London's best Thai restaurants. The surroundings resemble a tropical jungle, the perfect backdrop for excellent, beautifully prepared dishes presented by waiters in Thai costume. Excellent vegetarian menu. *LD (Reserve) open to 00.30, to 22.30 Sun.* A.Ax.Dc.V. **£££+**

Busabong Too   6 C4
1a Langton St SW10. 071-352 7414. Low tables and cushions to sit on. Very pleasant, attentive service. Fisherman's soup, beef satay, mint pork with water chestnuts. *LD (Reserve) open to 23.15.* A.Ax.Dc.V. **££**

VEGETARIAN & WHOLEFOOD

Many restaurants now cater for vegetarian tastes, with a variety of dishes on their menus. Below are two specialist establishments:

Cranks   4 D2
8 Marshall St W1. 071-437 9431. The original London health-food restaurant. Hot and cold vegetable dishes, soups, pies, salads, cakes, bread, and vegetable juices. Licensed. Other branches. *LD (Reserve D) open to 23.00. Closed Sun.* A.Ax.Dc.V. **££**

Diwana Bhel-Poori House   1 E5
121 Drummond St NW1. 071-387 5556. Also at 50 Westbourne Grove W2 (**3 C2**). 071-221 0721. Indian vegetarian food at very reasonable prices. Samosas, thalis, bhajis. *LD open to 23.45. Closed Mon.* A.Dc.V. **£**

VIETNAMESE

Mekong   7 C2
46 Churton St SW1. 071-630 9568. Sample a blend of Vietnamese and Chinese cuisine in this simple bistro-like restaurant. Spring rolls, beef with lemon grass and a variety of vegetarian dishes. Set menus. *LD (Reserve) open to 22.45.* A.V. **££**

Van Long   4 E2
40 Frith St W1. 071-434 3772. Attractive, modern Vietnamese

restaurant with pretty, pastel decor. The set menus can be helpful for the uninitiated. Excellent soups and seafood dishes, fried seaweed with scallops. *LD open to 23.30. Closed Sun.* A.Ax.Dc.V. **££**

Breakfast and brunch

Price symbols for this section only are as follows: **£** *under £5.00;* **££** *£5.00-£8.00;* **£££** *over £8.00.*

CAFÉS
Bar Italia   **4 E2**
22 Frith St W1. 071-437 4520. Authentic Italian café, serving breakfast all day. *Open 24 hrs Mon-Sun.* No credit cards. **£**
Bartholomew's   **5 C1**
57a West Smithfield EC1. 071-606 3903. Traditional English breakfast. *Open 07.00-11.00. Closed Sat & Sun.* A.Ax.Dc.V. **£**
The Hermitage   **1 G4**
19 Leigh St WC1. 071-387 8034. Friendly, stylish café. Baguettes, croissants, pain au chocolat. Newspapers provided. *Open 10.00-22.30.* A.Ax.V. **£**
Le Tire Bouchon   **4 D3**
6 Upper James St W1. 071-437 5348. Continental breakfast. *Open 08.30-21.15. Closed Sat & Sun.* A.Ax.Dc.V. **££**

HOTELS
Claridge's   **4 C3**
Brook St W1. 071-629 8860. English, à la carte or Continental. *Served 07.30-10.30.* A.Ax.Dc.V. **££-£££**
Hyde Park, Park Room   **4 A5**
66 Knightsbridge SW1. 071-235 2000. English, à la carte or Continental. *Served 07.00 (08.00 Sun & Bank hols)-10.30.* A.Ax.Dc.V. **£££**
Ritz   **4 D4**
Piccadilly W1. 071-493 8181. English, à la carte or Continental. *Served 07.00 (08.00 Sat & Sun)-10.30.* A.Ax.Dc.V. **£££**
Savoy   **4 G3**
Strand WC2. 071-836 4343. English or Continental. *Served 07.00 (08.00 Sun)-10.30.* A.Ax.Dc.V. **£££**

Afternoon tea

Afternoon tea is a British institution; at one time very fashionable, sociable, leisurely and gossipy. This list gives some of the remaining strongholds. Prices can vary but you should not normally expect to pay more than **£12.00** *for a full tea. Most will cost between* **£5.00-£10.00**.

HOTELS
Brown's   4 D3
Dover St W1. 071-493 6020. Very English, country house setting. Sandwiches, cakes, muffins. *Served 15.00-18.00.*

Claridge's   4 C3
Brook St W1. 071-629 8860. A touch of class in the comfortable reading room. Sandwiches, assorted pastries, cakes. *Served 15.00-17.30 (Reserve).*

Dorchester   4 B4
Park Lane W1. 071-629 8888. Dainty sandwiches, cakes and pastries in opulent surroundings. *Served 15.00-18.00.*

Ritz   4 D4
Piccadilly W1. 071-493 8181. Tea in the Palm Court, with dainty sandwiches, pastries and cream cakes. *Served 15.00 & 16.30 (Reserve Sat & Sun).*

DEPARTMENT STORES
Most large department stores provide afternoon tea but the following are among the best:
Fortnum & Mason   4 D4
181 Piccadilly W1. 071-734 8040. Afternoon tea is available at three locations in the store *Mon-Sat.* St James's Restaurant serves a set tea of sandwiches, scones, cake, tea or coffee to a piano accompaniment *15.00-17.20.* The Patio Bar and Soda Fountain offer an à la carte tea menu *14.30-17.30.*

Harrods Georgian Restaurant   3 G6
Knightsbridge SW1. 071-730 1234. Enjoy tea, sandwiches, coffee or fruit juice with bread and butter, scones, cakes and pastries; *served from 15.00.* Alternatively have tea on the Terrace; *served from 15.00.*

CAFÉS
Maison Bouquillon   3 C3
41 Moscow Rd W2. 071-727 0373. Over 50 varieties of cream cakes and pastries. Also hot savoury dishes, croissants. *Open 08.30-21.00 Mon-Sat, to 20.00 Sun.* No credit cards.

Maison Sagne   1 C6
105 Marylebone High St W1. 071-935 6240. Traditional tea shop with its own bakery and delicious pâtisserie. Coffee and croissants, lunches and tea. *Open 09.00-17.00, to 12.30 Sat. Closed Sun.* No credit cards.

Pâtisserie Valerie   4 E3
44 Old Compton St W1. 071-437 3466. Long-established Soho pâtisserie. Tea, coffee and hot chocolate accompany superb cakes and sandwiches. *Open 08.00-20.00 Mon-Fri, 08.00-19.00 Sat, 10.00-17.30 Sun.* No credit cards.

THÉ DANSANT
Waldorf Hotel 4 G3
Aldwych WC2. 071-836 2400. Opulent Palm Court tea lounge
with comfort and good service. Edwardian elegance. Dancing
to the band and full set tea *Sat & Sun 15.30-18.30 (Reserve).*

Brasseries

Here is a selection of establishments serving food all day
(from breakfast to full meals):
La Brasserie 3 F6
272 Brompton Rd SW3. 071-584 1688. Probably one of the
closest things to a real French brasserie in London.
Conventional menu with omelettes, croque monsieur; also
breakfast and pâtisseries. *Open 08.00-24.00 Mon-Sat, 10.00-
23.30 Sun.* A.Ax.Dc.V. **£££**
Covent Garden Brasserie 4 F3
1 Covent Garden Piazza WC2. 071-240 6654. Relaxed
atmosphere at this Parisian style brasserie. Breakfast and
afternoon tea as well as light meals and more substantial
dishes. *Open 12.00-23.00 Mon-Fri, 11.00-23.00 Sat & Sun.*
A.Ax.Dc.V. **££**
The Dôme 6 D4
354 King's Rd SW3. 071-352 7611. One of a chain of French-
style brasseries based on the Paris Dôme. Coffee, wine,
spirits, beer and good food from breakfast and pâtisseries to
steak sandwiches. *Open 08.00-23.00 Mon-Sat, 09.00-22.30
Sun.* A.Ax.Dc.V. **££**
Soho Soho 4 E2
11-13 Frith St W1. 071-494 3491. A brasserie/wine bar with a
selection of good value wines. Brasserie offers typical French
menu with croque monsieur etc; Rôtisserie downstairs offers
grills and snacks all day. *Open 12.00-23.00. Closed Sun.*
A.Ax.Dc.V. **££**
Tuttons Brasserie 4 F3
11-12 Russell St WC2. 071-836 4141. Right on the edge of
Covent Garden piazza, this is a large, airy brasserie with a
relaxed atmosphere. Good reasonably priced English/interna-
tional menu. *Open 09.30-23.30 Mon-Thur & Sun, to 24.00 Fri
& Sat.* A.Ax.Dc.V. **£**

Wine bars

Most wine bars are open pub hours: 11.00/11.30-15.00 &
17.30-23.00 Mon-Sat; 12.00-14.00 & 19.00-22.30 Sun. *Some
are open all day:* 11.00-23.00 Mon-Sat; 12.00-14.00 & 19.00-
22.30 Sun. *These are denoted by* ◗.

Most offer cold food (such as sandwiches) all day, and bar food (anything from pâté to steak) at designated times at lunchtime and in the evening.
L = 12.00/12.30-14.30/15.00.
D = 18.00-22.30/23.00.
all day = throughout the day from lunchtime to last orders in the evening.
Nicholson's London Pub Guide *gives more detailed information on brasseries and wine bars in the capital.*

Andrew Edmunds   4 D3
46 Lexington St W1. 071-437 5708. Small, charming wine bar/ restaurant with tempting daily specials to complement an excellent wine list. *L.*

🍷 Archduke   5 B4
Concert Hall Approach, South Bank SE1. 071-928 9370. Nestling underneath the arches near Waterloo Station, with pleasant green decor, live jazz and good food. The restaurant specialises in sausages from around the world. *L D.*

🍷 L'Artiste Musclé   4 C4
1 Shepherd Market W1. 071-493 6150. Informal, French wine bar. Good food with daily specials chalked up on the blackboard. Reasonably priced, mainly French, wines. Tables outside in *summer. L D.*

Balls Bros
One of the oldest wine bar chains in London. Very popular, with most of its branches in the City. Over 60 wines on their list, plus wines by the glass. All the following serve food *lunchtime* and *evening.* NB: All branches *close early at 20.30/21.00 and are closed Sat & Sun.* The following is only a selection:

🍷 Hay's Galleria, Tooley St SE1. 071-407 4301.   **5 F4**
3 Budge Row, Cannon St EC4. 071-248 7557. *L only.*   **5 D2**
2 Old Change Court, St Paul's Churchyard EC4.   **5 D2**
071-248 8697.
St Mary-at-Hill EC3. 071-626 0321.   **5 F3**
6 Cheapside EC2. 071-248 2708.   **5 D2**

🍷 Bill Bentley's Wine Bar   3 G6
31 Beauchamp Place SW3. 071-589 5080. Dark, cosy bar with an old-fashioned interior and an excellent fish restaurant upstairs. Snacks from the oyster bar and a reasonably priced wine list. *L. Closed Sun.*

🍷 Bow Wine Vaults   5 D2
10 Bow Churchyard EC4. 071-248 1121. Victorian bar within the sound of Bow Bells. Popular with City gents, with a good selection of over 100 French, Californian, Spanish and German wines. Imaginative food. *L only.* Bar snacks area with free snacks *from 17.30-20.00. Closed Sat & Sun.*

🍷 **Brahms & Liszt**   **4 F3**
19 Russell St WC2. 071-240 3661. Lively, crowded wine bar with loud music and a friendly atmosphere. Good food and a reasonable selection of wines. Food *all day.*

Café des Amis du Vin   **4 F3**
11-14 Hanover Place WC2. 071-379 3444. Close to the Royal Opera House and always busy. Good range of French, German and Spanish wines accompanied by an inventive menu. *L D. Closed Sun.*

Cork & Bottle   **4 E3**
44-46 Cranbourn St WC2. 071-734 7807. Spacious basement wine bar with an unusual variety of quality wines. *L D.*

🍷 **Crusting Pipe**   **4 F3**
27 Covent Garden Piazza WC2. 071-836 1415. Part of the Davy's chain. Very popular with seating outside under the piazza canopy. Grills and daily specials in the restaurant and very friendly, helpful service. Food *all day.*

Davy's Wine Bars
Old prints and sawdust-covered floors create a bygone Victorian image in these wine bars, the names of which date back to the wine trade of 100 years ago. NB: Most branches *close early at around 20.30 and are closed Sat & Sun.* The following is only a selection:

Boot & Flogger   **5 D5**
10-20 Redcross Way SE1. 071-407 1184. Food *all day.*

Bung Hole   **4 G1**
57 High Holborn WC1. 071-242 4318. *L.*

City Boot   **5 E1**
7 Moorfields High Walk EC2. 071-628 2360. *L.*

Dover Street Wine Bar   **4 C3**
8-9 Dover St W1. 071-629 9813. A basement wine bar with a friendly atmosphere and a very good selection of wines. Live music. Open late for real night owls! *L D to 01.30. Open to 03.00. Closed Sat L & Sun.*

🍷 **Ebury Wine Bar**   **7 A2**
139 Ebury St SW1. 071-730 5447. Crowded and cramped, but with a pleasant atmosphere. Comprehensive wine list. *L D.*

🍷 **Gordon's**   **4 F4**
47 Villiers St WC1. 071-930 1408. 200-year-old wine bar in curved, cavernous undervaults. Excellent selection of wines and sherries. Good food. *L D.*

🍷 **Shampers**   **4 D3**
4 Kingly St W1. 071-437 1692. A brasserie and wine bar with a congenial atmosphere and fine selection of wines. Good, imaginative menu. *L D.*

El Vino   **5 B2**
47 Fleet St EC4. 071-353 6786. Something of an institution.

Thoroughly masculine atmosphere popular with local lawyers and still adhering to a dress code – men in jacket and tie and women in dresses/skirts. Long and famous wine list. *L. Open to 20.00. Closed Sat & Sun.*

Pubs

Some pubs still operate under the following opening hours: 11.00/11.30-15.00 & 17.30-23.00 Mon-Sat; 12.00-14.00 & 19.00-22.30 Sun. *Others are open all day* 11.00-23.00 Mon-Sat; 12.00-14.00 & 19.00-22.30 Sun. *These are denoted by* ☕. *Most pubs serve sandwiches and cold snacks all day, but hot food at designated times at lunchtime and in the evening.*
In the following section:
Bar food = ploughmans, salads, sandwiches, pies, lasagne.
Restaurant = three-course menu and more substantial dishes.
L = 12.30-14.30.
D = 17.30-21.00/22.00.
Nicholson's *London Pub Guide gives more detailed information on where to drink in the capital.*

The Cartoonist   **5 B2**
76 Shoe Lane EC4. 071-353 2828. In the heart of the old newspaper world, this Victorian pub is the headquarters of the International Cartoonist Club and is wallpapered with cartoons! *Bar food L. Closed Sat & Sun.*

☕ **Cheshire Cheese**   **5 B3**
5 Little Essex St WC2. 071-836 2347. Intimate Jacobean pub with original beams and three bars. Regulars come from the nearby Law Courts and it is reputedly haunted by an unfriendly ghost! *Bar food L. Closed Sat & Sun.*

☕ **Dirty Dick's**   **5 F2**
202 Bishopsgate EC2. 071-283 5888. The original pub named after Nat Bentley, well-known 18thC miser of the ballad. The cobwebs, stuffed cats and other detritus have since been removed with the remnants preserved behind glass. Now fully refurbished and serving real ales. *Bar food L. Restaurant L.*

The Flask
77 Highgate West Hill N6. 081-340 7260. Famous 17thC tavern named after the flasks bought here and filled at the Hampstead wells. Dick Turpin once hid in the cellars. Former patrons include Hogarth and Karl Marx. *Bar food L D. Restaurant L.*

☕ **French House**   **4 E2**
49 Dean St W1. 071-437 2799. Refuge for the Free French during World War II. De Gaulle drank here, as have Maurice Chevalier, Brendan Behan and Dylan Thomas. Excellent choice of wines and champagnes. *Bar food L D. Restaurant L D.*

🍺 George Inn   5 D5
77 Borough High St SE1. 071-407 2056. Unique galleried coaching inn rebuilt 1676 and featured in Dickens' *Little Dorrit*. Courtyard entertainment (usually Shakespeare) in *summer*. *Bar food L D. Restaurant L D.*

Holly Bush
22 Holly Mount, off Heath St NW3. 071-435 2892. Picturesque and rambling pub dating to 1796. Unchanged atmosphere prevails with gas lamps and a dark, sagging ceiling. *Bar food L.*

Island Queen   2 D3
87 Noel Rd N1. 071-226 5507. Looming papier mâché figures dominate the bar in this popular local. Pool room and restaurant. *Bar food L.*

The Lamb   2 B5
94 Lamb's Conduit St WC1. 071-405 0713. A busy Bloomsbury local with some intriguing music-hall photographs and Hogarth prints. Original snob-screens. *Bar food L. Restaurant Sun L.*

🍺 Lamb & Flag   4 F3
33 Rose St WC2. 071-497 9504. 300-year-old pub originally called the 'Bucket of Blood' because of the occurrence of bare fist fights. Now a popular, mellow bar. Fine range of cheeses. *Bar food L.*

Old Bull & Bush
North End Way NW3. 081-455 3685. The famous pub of the Florrie Forde song. Drink on the forecourt and gaze at Hampstead Heath opposite. *Bar food L. Restaurant L.*

Running Footman   4 C4
5 Charles St W1. 071-499 2988. Once had the longest name in London, 'I am the only Running Footman' (after the men who used to run before carriages, clearing the way and paying the tolls). Popular with nearby workers. *Bar food L D. Restaurant D.*

🍺 The Salisbury   4 F3
90 St Martin's Lane WC2. 071-836 5863. Glittering Edwardian pub in the heart of theatreland. Cut-glass mirrors and first-class hot and cold buffet. Famous meeting place for theatre people. *Bar food L D.*

Seven Stars   5 B2
53 Carey St WC2. 071-242 8521. Behind the Law Courts stands this early 17thC pub, one of the smallest in London. *Bar food L.*

🍺 Sherlock Holmes   4 F4
10 Northumberland St WC2. 071-930 2644. Upstairs is a perfect replica of Holmes' study at 221b Baker St. *Bar food L D.*

🍺 Spaniard's Inn
Spaniard's Rd NW3. 071-455 3276. Famous 16thC inn with literary and Dick Turpin associations. Pretty garden. *Bar food L D.*

Still & Star   5 G2
1 Little Somerset St (off Mansell St) E1. 071-488 3761. The

only one of its name in England, and set in 'blood alley' where Jack the Ripper struck. *Bar food L.*

RIVERSIDE PUBS
🍺 The Anchor   5 C3
Bankside SE1. 071-407 1577. 18thC replacement of original destroyed by Great Fire of 1666. Exposed beams, large open fireplace. *Bar food L D. Restaurant L D (Reserve).*

The Angel
101 Bermondsey Wall East SE16. 071-237 3608. 15thC Thames-side pub with extensive views of Tower Bridge, the City and the Pool of London. Famous former imbibers include Samuel Pepys, Captain Cook and Laurel and Hardy. *Bar food L (not Sat) D. Restaurant L (not Sat) D.*

Bull's Head
Strand-on-the-Green W4. 081-994 0647. 350-year-old Chiswick waterfront tavern. Cromwell was nearly caught here by the Royalists. Sheltered beer garden and terrace. *Bar food L D. Restaurant L (not Sun & Mon) D.*

🍺 Cutty Sark
Ballast Quay, Lassell St SE10. 081-858 3146. Quiet Georgian pub with wooden interior. Overlooks the river and wharves near *Cutty Sark* in dry dock. *Bar food L.*

🍺 Dickens Inn   5 G4
St Katharine's Way E1. 071-488 2208. Converted historic warehouse with fine views of the diverse craft in St Katharine's Dock marina. Outside eating in *summer*. Two restaurants. *Bar food L D. Restaurant L D.*

🍺 The Dove
19 Upper Mall W6. 081-748 5405. Mellow 18thC pub with terrace overlooking the river. Graham Greene and Ernest Hemingway drank here. Has the smallest bar room, which has earned it an entry in the *Guinness Book of Records*. *Bar food L. Restaurant L.*

London Apprentice
62 Church St, Old Isleworth, Middx. 081-560 1915. Famous 16thC pub with fine Elizabethan and Georgian interiors. Prints of Hogarth's *Apprentices*. *Bar food L. Restaurant L.*

🍺 The Mayflower
117 Rotherhithe St SE16. 071-237 4088. Partially rebuilt Tudor inn named after the ship in which the Pilgrim Fathers reached America. The only pub in England licensed to sell British and American stamps. Drink on the jetty in good weather. *Bar food L D. Restaurant L D.*

Prospect of Whitby
57 Wapping Wall E1. 071-481 1095. Historic dockland tavern dating back to the reign of Henry VIII. Samuel Pepys drank

here, as did 'hanging' Judge Jeffreys. Decorated with nautical souvenirs and fine pewter. Restaurant overlooking the river. *Bar food L D. Restaurant L D.*

MUSIC PUBS

These vary enormously from pubs with a pianist playing old favourites to those with large audience space for live bands. The pubs listed below are established live music venues. It's always advisable to check listings in advance to find out what is on. Most pubs with a separate music room charge an entry fee, though it is rarely more than £5.00 and often less.

Bull & Gate
389 Kentish Town Rd NW5. 071-485 5358. Rock, reggae and soul. *Evenings Mon-Sun. Bar food L.*

● Bull's Head
373 Lonsdale Rd SW13. 081-876 5241. Mainstream modern jazz by top English and international musicians. *Evenings Mon-Sun & Sun lunchtime. Bar food L D. Restaurant L (Sun only) D.*

Half Moon
93 Lower Richmond Rd SW15. 081-788 2387. Jazz, R & B, rock, folk and soul in separate back room. Occasional top names. *Bar food D.*

Swan Tavern   6 A5
1 Fulham Broadway SW6. 071-385 1840. Mixed bands and R & B *evenings Mon-Sun & Sun lunchtime. Bar food D.*

White Lion   3 E4
37 Central St EC1. 071-253 4975. Traditional East End pub where you can sing along to the piano played *Sat & Sun evenings. Bar food L D.*

THEATRE PUBS

Gate at the Prince Albert   3 B3
12 Pembridge Rd W11. 071-229 0706. New works, adaptations of novels and revivals of lesser known plays by important writers. Performances *Mon-Sat.*

King's Head   2 D3
115 Upper St N1. 071-226 1916. Probably the best known and most widely reviewed of the theatre pubs. Decorated with theatre bills. You can have a meal before the show and stay at your table for the performance. Also live music. Performances *Mon-Sun. Bar food L. Restaurant D.*

Latchmere Theatre   6 F6
503 Battersea Park Rd SW11. 071-223 3549. Good reputation for plays, cabaret and revues. Check listings in *Time Out* or *What's On* for late-night shows and Sunday performances. Performances *Mon-Sun. Bar food L D. Restaurant L D.*

ENTERTAINMENT

For more detailed information see Nicholson's London
Nightlife Guide.
Artsline: *071-388 2227 offers free advice and information on
access to arts and entertainment for disabled people.*
Curtain Call: *(0891) 888788 is a 24-hr entertainment information service giving previews and reviews of theatre, dance,
musicals and opera.*

Theatre ticket agencies

Fenchurch Booking Agency   **5 D4**
94 Southwark St SE1. 071-928 8585. A.V.
First Call
071-240 7200. A.Ax.Dc.V.
Keith Prowse
071-379 9901. A.Ax.Dc.V.
Society of West End Theatre Half-Price   **4 E3**
Ticket Booth (SWET)
Leicester Sq WC2. Unsold tickets at half price on the day of the
performance from the pavilion on the south side of Leicester
Square. *Open from 12.00* (for matinées) *& 14.30-18.30* (for
evening performances). Maximum 4 tickets. No credit cards.
Ticketmaster UK Ltd   **4 F3**
78 St Martin's Lane WC2. 071-379 4444.

Theatres

Adelphi   **4 F3**
Strand WC2. 071-836 7611. Musicals including the long-run-
ning *Me and My Girl*.
Albery   **4 F3**
St Martin's Lane WC2. 071-867 1115. Originally the New
Theatre. Renamed in 1973. Musicals, comedy and drama.
Aldwych   **4 G3**
Aldwych WC2. 071-836 6404. Former London home of the
Royal Shakespeare Company. Plays, comedies and musicals.
Ambassadors   **4 E3**
West St WC2. 071-836 6111. Small theatre, the original home
of *The Mousetrap* until it moved to the nearby St Martin's.
Apollo   **4 E3**
Shaftesbury Ave W1. 071-494 5070. Old tradition of musical
comedy. Now presents musicals, comedy and drama.

Apollo Victoria 4 C6

17 Wilton Rd SW1. 071-828 8665. This auditorium was completely transformed to accommodate the hit rollerskating railway musical *Starlight Express*.

Barbican 2 E6

Barbican Centre, Silk St EC2. 071-638 8891. Purpose-built for the Royal Shakespeare Company; the main auditorium is for large-scale productions in repertory and the Pit, a smaller studio theatre, is for new works.

Comedy 4 E3

Panton St SW1. 071-867 1045. Good intimate theatre showing unusual comedy and small-cast plays.

Criterion 4 E3

Piccadilly Circus W1. 071-930 0314. Listed building recently re-opened after extensive renovations. Houses the only underground auditorium in London.

Drury Lane (Theatre Royal) 4 G3

Catherine St WC2. 071-494 5062. Operated under Royal Charter by Thomas Kiligrew in 1663, it has been burnt or pulled down and rebuilt four times. Nell Gwynne performed here and Orange Moll sold her oranges. Garrick, Mrs Siddons, Kean and others played here. General policy now is vast musical productions like *Miss Saigon*.

Duchess 4 G3

Catherine St WC2. 071-494 5075. Opened 1929. Plays, serious drama, light comedy and musicals.

Duke of York's 4 F3

St Martin's Lane WC2. 071-836 5122. Built by 'Mad (Violet) Melnotte' in 1892. Associated with names like Frohman, George Bernard Shaw, Granville Barker, Chaplin and the Ballet Rambert. Refurbished by the present owners, Capital Radio, for major productions.

Fortune 4 F3

Russell St WC2. 071-836 2238. Small compared with its neighbour, Drury Lane. Intimate revues (Peter Cook and Dudley Moore shot to fame here in *Beyond the Fringe*), musicals and modern drama.

Garrick 4 E2

Charing Cross Rd WC2. 071-494 5085. Built 1897. Notable managers included Bouchier and Jack Buchanan.

Globe 4 E3

Shaftesbury Ave W1. 071-494 5065. A wide variety of successful plays and comedies. The third theatre of this name in London.

Greenwich

Crooms Hill SE10. 081-858 7755. Stages a season of eight plays annually including new works, revivals and classics,

THEATRES

Adelphi 836 7611
Albery 867 1115
Aldwych 836 6404
Ambassadors 836 1171
Apollo 494 5070
Apollo Victoria 828 8665
Arts 836 2132
Bloomsbury 387 9629
Cambridge 379 5299
Comedy 867 1045
Criterion 839 4488
Dominion 580 9562
Duchess 494 5075
Duke of York's 836 5122
Fortune 836 2238
Garrick 494 5085
Globe 494 5065
Her Majesty's 494 5400
ICA 930 3647
London Coliseum 836 3161
London Palladium
  494 5020
Lyric 494 5045
Mermaid 410 0000
New London 405 0072
Old Vic 928 7616
Palace 434 0909
Phoenix 867 1044

Piccadilly 867 1118
Players 839 1134
Players 839 1134
Prince Edward 734 8951
Prince of Wales 839 5987
Queen's 494 5040
Royal Court 730 1745
Royal Festival Hall
  928 8800
Royal National 928 2252
Royal Opera House
  240 1066
Royalty 494 5090
St. Martin's 836 1443
Savoy 836 8888
Shaftesbury 379 5399
Strand 930 8800
Theatre Royal, Drury Lane
  494 5000
Theatre Royal, Haymarket
  930 8800
Vaudeville 836 9987
Victoria Palace 834 1317
Whitehall 867 1119
Wigmore Hall 935 2141
Wyndham's 867 1116
Young Vic 928 6363

CINEMAS

Astral 734 6387
Curzon Mayfair 465 8865
Curzon Phoenix 240 9661
Curzon West End 439 4805
Empire 437 1234
ICA 930 3647
Lumière 836 0691
MGM Haymarket 839
MGM Oxford St 636 0310
MGM Panton St 930 0631
MGM Piccadilly 437 3561
MGM Shaftesbury Ave
  836 6279
MGM Swiss Centre
  439 4470
MGM Tottenham Court Rd
  636 6148
MGM Trocadero
  434 0031

Metro 437 0757
Minema 235 4225
National Film Theatre
  928 3232
Odeon Haymarket
  839 7697
Odeon Leicester Sq
  930 6111
Odeon Marble Arch
  723 2011
Odeon Mezzanine (Odeon
  Leicester Sq) 930 6111
Odeon West End
  930 5252
Plaza 437 1234
Prince Charles 437 8181
Renoir 837 8402
Warner West End
  (Temporarily closed)

WEST END
THEATRES & CINEMAS

● Theatres
● Cinemas

Not to scale

© Nicholson

often with famous names in the cast. Bar and good restaurant.

Haymarket (Theatre Royal) 4 E3
Haymarket SW1. 071-930 8800. Originally built in 1721 as the Little Theatre in the Hay, it became Royal 50 years later. The present theatre was built by Nash in 1821 and is sometimes enlivened by the ghost of Mr Buckstone, Queen Victoria's favourite actor-manager. He no doubt approves of the policy to present plays of quality.

Her Majesty's 4 E3
Haymarket SW1. 071-494 5050. A fine Victorian baroque theatre founded by Beerbohm Tree. Successes include *West Side Story, Fiddler on the Roof, Amadeus* and, most recently, Lloyd Webber's *Phantom of the Opera*.

Lyric 4 E3
Shaftesbury Ave W1. 071-494 5045. Oldest theatre in Shaftesbury Avenue (built 1888). Eleonora Duse, Sarah Bernhardt, Owen Nares and Tallulah Bankhead all had long runs here.

Lyric Hammersmith
King St W6. 081-741 2311. Rebuilt and restored to original Victorian splendour inside a modern shell. Spacious foyers, bar, restaurant and terrace. Wide-ranging productions.

Mermaid 5 C3
Puddle Dock, Blackfriars EC4. 071-410 0000. Plays and musicals. Restaurant and two bars overlooking the Thames.

New London 4 F2
Drury Lane WC2. 071-405 0072. Can convert from a 900-seat conventional theatre to an intimate theatre-in-the-round within minutes. Built on the site of the old Winter Gardens. The hit musical *Cats* is well-established here.

Old Vic 5 B5
Waterloo Rd SE1. 071-928 7616. Built 1818. For a long time the home of the National Theatre Company, then housed the Prospect Theatre Company. It now shows plays and musicals amid recreated Victorian decor.

Palace 4 E3
Shaftesbury Ave W1. 071-434 0909. Listed building. Originally intended by Richard D'Oyly Carte to be the Royal English Opera House, but eventually became the Palace Theatre of Varieties. Staged performances by Pavlova and Nijinski. Now owned by Sir Andrew Lloyd Webber whose musical *Jesus Christ Superstar* enjoyed a record run here; *Les Miserables* is its latest success story.

Phoenix 4 E2
Charing Cross Rd WC2. 071-867 1044. A large theatre showing comedies, plays and musicals.

Piccadilly   **4 D3**
Denman St W1. 071-867 1118. A pre-war theatre which
showed the first season of 'Talkies' in Britain. Varied post-
war history of light comedy, plays and musicals. Many Royal
Shakespeare Company productions are staged here.

Playhouse   **4 F4**
Northumberland Ave WC2. 071-839 4401. Edwardian theatre
used as a BBC studio and then closed in 1975. Restored to
former glory and re-opened in 1987. Stages musicals, serious
drama and comedies.

Prince Edward   **4 E3**
Old Compton St W1. 071-734 8951. Started life as the 'London
Casino' in 1936, then became a cinema. Now a large theatre
staging musicals; the hit show *Evita* ran for 2900 performances
here.

Prince of Wales   **4 E3**
Coventry St W1. 071-839 5972. Rebuilt 1937, this large,
modern theatre has housed many musicals.

Queen's   **4 E3**
Shaftesbury Ave W1. 071-494 5040. Very successful between
the wars. Still presents good drama and varied productions.

Royal Court   **6 F2**
Sloane Sq SW1. 071-730 1745. Home of the English Stage
Company, which produces many major experimental plays.

Royal National   **5 A4**
South Bank SE1. 071-928 2252. Complex of three theatres,
the Olivier, Lyttelton and Cottesloe. Home of the National
Theatre Company. Stages a wide mixture of plays in repertory,
including new works, revivals, Shakespeare and musicals.
Also free foyer entertainment. Restaurants, bars, exhibitions.

St Martin's   **4 E3**
West St WC2. 071-836 1443. Intimate playhouse with unusual
polished teak doors. *The Mousetrap* continues its record run
here having transferred from the Ambassadors.

Savoy   **4 G3**
Strand WC2. 071-836 8888. Entrance is in the forecourt of
the Savoy Hotel. Produces a variety of plays, comedies and
musicals. *Temporarily closed due to fire damage.*

Shaftesbury   **4 E3**
Shaftesbury Ave WC2. 071-379 5399. Permanent base of the
Theatre of Comedy Company.

Strand   **4 G3**
Aldwych WC2. 071-930 8800. Large theatre presenting a
mixture of straight plays, comedies and musicals.

Vaudeville   **4 F3**
Strand WC2. 071-836 9987. Listed building which originally ran
farce and burlesque (hence the name), then became straight,
which for the most part it remains.

Victoria Palace
4 D6

Victoria St SW1. 071-834 1317. Musicals, variety shows and plays. Once home of the Crazy Gang and the *Black and White Minstrel Show*, the musical *Buddy* is a recent success.

Whitehall
4 F4

14 Whitehall SW1. 071-867 1119. Splendid art deco interior. Now one of the Wyndham Theatres group staging varied productions.

Wyndham's
4 E2

Charing Cross Rd WC2. 071-867 1116. Small, pretty and successful theatre founded by Sir Charles Wyndham, the famous actor-manager. Plays, comedies and musicals.

Young Vic
5 B5

66 The Cut SE1. 071-938 6363. Young people's repertoire theatre mainly showing the classics and established modern plays, but also some new plays and musicals.

Open-air theatre

Various parks stage one-off theatrical events in summer. *To find out more about these, check* Time Out *and* What's On *or phone the individual park (see* Out and About *on page 61).*

Holland Park Theatre
3 A5

Holland Park W8. 071-602 7856. 600-seat theatre staging dance, opera and theatre productions *Jun-Aug.* Canopy covering is a definite attraction given the fickleness of the English summer! *Phone for times and days.*

Regent's Park Open-Air Theatre
1 C4

Inner Circle, Regent's Park NW1. 071-486 2431. Enclosed within the park, in a magical setting. Plays by Shakespeare (*A Midsummer Night's Dream* is a perennial favourite) and others alternate from *May-Sep.* Book in advance. *Performances 20.00 Mon-Sat and 14.30 Wed, Thur & Sat.*

Opera, ballet and dance

London Coliseum
4 F3

St Martin's Lane WC2. 071-836 3161. London's biggest theatre – 2356 seats. A leading national music venue, home of the English National Opera and a favourite with visiting foreign companies. Dance and ballet productions are staged in *summer*, opera at other times. Box office *open 10.00-20.00. Closed Sun.* A.Ax.Dc.V.

The Place
1 F4

17 Duke's Rd WC1. 071-387 0031. One of the most innovative and modern dance venues. It is home to the London Contemporary Dance School and London Contemporary Dance Theatre, which stages interestingly choreographed productions. Box office *open 12.00-18.00, or up until time of performance.* A.V.

Royal Opera House   **4 F3**
Covent Garden WC2. 071-240 1066. Recorded information:
071-836 6903. Credit card booking: (0898) 600001. The home
of the Royal Ballet and the Royal Opera Company is the most
lavish theatre in London and the greatest stage for British
opera and ballet. Sixty-five tickets are reserved for sale at the
box office in Floral St from *10.00* on day of performance only
(except for gala performances). If the performance is a sell-
out, 50 standing-room tickets are made available in the foyer
at *19.00*. Be warned – queues have been known to start at
dawn! Box office *open 10.00-20.00. Closed Sun*. A.Ax.Dc.V.

Sadler's Wells   **2 C4**
Rosebery Ave EC1. 071-278 8916. The first theatre here was
a 'musick' house built in 1683 by Thomas Sadler as a side
attraction to his medicinal well. Birthplace of the English
National Opera, it now stages productions by leading British and
international ballet, dance and opera companies. Box office
open 10.30-19.30, or 18.30 if no performance. A.Ax.Dc.V.

Concert halls

Barbican Hall   **2 E6**
Barbican Centre EC1. 071-638 8891. Base of the London
Symphony Orchestra. Three one-month seasons per year.
Also used as a venue for opera, jazz, and light classical music.
Box office *open 09.00-20.00 Mon-Sun*. A.Ax.V.

Central Hall   **4 E5**
Storey's Gate SW1. 071-222 8010. This ornate building is the
Chief Methodist Church, built 1905-11. Large hall seats 2640
and is used for organ recitals and orchestral concerts. Buy tickets at door; or direct from event organisers. *Phone for details*.

Conway Hall   **2 B6**
Red Lion Sq WC1. 071-242 8032. Two halls, one of which is
famous for hosting celebrated *Sun eve* chamber music concerts from *Oct-Apr*. No telephone box office. No credit cards.

Purcell Room   **5 A4**
South Bank SE1. 071-928 8800. Smallest of the three South
Bank concert halls. Popular and ideal for chamber music and solo
concerts. Box office *open 10.00-21.00 Mon-Sun*. A.Ax.Dc.V.

Queen Elizabeth Hall   **5 A4**
South Bank SE1. 071-928 8800. Shares a foyer with the
Purcell Room. Seats 1100, and usually stages chamber music,
small orchestral concerts or solo recitals. Box office *open
10.00-21.00 Mon-Sun*. A.Ax.Dc.V.

Royal Albert Hall   **3 E5**
Kensington Gore SW7. 071-589 8212. Victorian domed hall
used for rock, folk and jazz but especially for classical con-

certs. Famous for the annual Promenade concerts from *Jul-Sep* (see page 50). Box office *open 09.00-21.00 Mon-Sun.* A.V.

Royal Festival Hall 5 A4

South Bank SE1. 071-928 8800. Built in 1951 for the Festival of Britain, it seats 3000 and hosts mainly choral and orchestral concerts. Box office *open 10.00-21.00 Mon-Sun.* A.Ax.Dc.V.

Wigmore Hall 4 C2

36 Wigmore St W1. 071-935 2141. Excellent acoustics and intimate atmosphere. Popular coffee concerts *11.30 Sun.* Stages instrumental, song, chamber music and solo recitals. Seats 540. Box office *open 10.00-20.30 Mon-Sun (telephone bookings until 19.00).* A.Ax.Dc.V.

Dinner and entertainment

Dine in elegant surroundings with cabaret entertainment and dancing at one of the following venues. In most cases it is advisable to book in advance.

Barbarella 1 6 B5

428 Fulham Rd SW6. 071-385 9434. Cascading fountains, plus a stylish, sophisticated disco. Unusual Italian menu. *D open to 03.00. Closed Sun.* A.Ax.Dc.V. **£££**

Entrecôte 4 F1

124a Southampton Row WC1. 071-405 1466. Romantic, candlelit atmosphere, with a wide-ranging international menu. Resident dance band plays *from 21.00 Fri & Sat. Open to 23.45, to 22.45 Sun.* A.Ax.Dc.V. **£££**

L'Hirondelle 4 D3

99-101 Regent St W1 (entrance in Swallow St). 071-734 1511. Theatre/restaurant with spectacular, glamorous cabaret. International menu. Live music *from 21.30. Cabaret 23.00 & 01.30. Open to 02.00. Closed Sun.* A.Ax.Dc.V. **£££**

Royal Garden Hotel, Royal Roof Restaurant 3 C5

2-24 Kensington High St W8. 071-937 8000. Modern European restaurant with dinner dancing *Thur-Sat evening.* Excellent views over Kensington Palace and Gardens. *Open to 22.30, to 23.00 Sat. Closed Sun.* A.Ax.Dc.V. **£££**+

Savoy Restaurant 4 G3

Savoy Hotel, Strand WC2. 071-836 4343. Elegant and formal, overlooking the Thames. Worldwide and well-deserved reputation. Dancing to the resident trio. *D open to 23.30. Closed Sun.* A.Ax.Dc.V. **£££**+

Talk of London 4 F2

Drury Lane WC2. 081-568 1616. Modern theatre/restaurant featuring some of London's most popular cabaret acts, including music from Andrew Lloyd Webber musicals and other West End hit shows. Dancing to a resident band. French and international cooking. *Open to 24.00.* A.Ax.Dc.V. **£££**+

Terrace Restaurant   4 B4
Dorchester Hotel, Park Lane W1. 071-629 8888. Stately dinner dancing in gracious surroundings. French *haute cuisine. Open to 01.00. Closed Sun.* A.Ax.Dc.V. **£££**

Terrazza Est   5 B2
109 Fleet St EC4. 071-353 2680. Large basement restaurant known as the Spaghetti Opera for its superb, uplifting opera singing *(from 19.30).* Lively atmosphere. Set and à la carte menus. *Open to 23.00. Closed Sat & Sun.* A.Ax.Dc.V. **££**

Villa dei Cesari   7 C4
135 Grosvenor Rd SW1. 071-828 7453. Fine views of the Thames from this converted riverside warehouse themed on the Roman Empire. Classical decor, latinised menu and waiters in tunics. Dancing to resident band. *Open to 02.30. Closed Mon.* A.Ax.Dc.V. **£££+**

Windows on the World, Hilton Hotel   4 B4
Park Lane W1. 071-493 8000. The name is not an exaggeration! Diners are afforded intoxicating views over the city from 28 floors up. Excellent French cooking. Dance floor, live music. *Open to 02.00.* A.Ax.Dc.V. **£££**

Live music venues

Consult Time Out, What's On *and the music press to check who's playing where, and when.*

Hammersmith Apollo
Queen Caroline St W6. 081-741 4868. Formerly the Hammersmith Odeon, this legendary venue plays host to all kinds of bands. Box office *open 11.00-20.00. Closed Sun.* No credit cards.

100 Club   4 C2
100 Oxford St W1. 071-636 0933. Friendly and comfortable basement club, historically the home of British traditional jazz. Also modern jazz, blues and swing. *Open to 24.00, to 03.00 Fri, to 01.00 Sat.* No box office. No credit cards.

Marquee   4 E2
105 Charing Cross Rd WC2. 071-437 6603. One of London's original rock clubs. Still a popular, lively spot. *Open to 24.00, to 03.00 Thur-Sat, to 22.30 Sun.* Box office *open 10.00-18.00 Mon-Fri, 12.00-18.00 Sat.* A.V.

Palookaville   4 F3
13a James St WC2. 071-240 5857. Lively restaurant and wine bar in the heart of Covent Garden. Bistro-style food accompanied by traditional or modern jazz. *Open to 01.30.* A.Ax.Dc.V.

Rock Garden   4 F3
6-7 Covent Garden Piazza WC2. 071-240 3961. Beneath the restaurant of the same name, a selection of starry-eyed young bands play in a converted banana warehouse. You might hear

tomorrow's stars – U2 and Dire Straits once played here. *Open to 03.00, to 24.00 Sun. A.Ax.V.*

Ronnie Scott's   **4 E2**
47 Frith St W1. 071-439 0747. Reputedly the best jazz club in London. Can be hot, smoky and sleazy on a busy night, but it's the sounds people come for. Advisable to book in advance. *Open to 03.00. Box office open 11.00-18.00 Mon-Fri, 12.30-18.00 Sat, from 19.00 Sun. A.Ax.Dc.V.*

Members-only clubs and casinos

To join an exclusive clientele in a relaxed and well-tended setting, choose one of the members-only nightclubs. Most of these will provide restaurants and entertainment. Be on your guard, however, for those which also offer 'hostesses' – women employed to boost the sales of drinks. Most of them have an expensive taste in champagne and you will have to pay for the pleasure of their company.

*Most clubs will require you to be a member, although short-term membership is usually available for visitors. In some clubs visitors from overseas get reduced rates or free membership. For an annual subscription fee the **Clubman's Club**, 262-264 Albemarle St W1 (071-287 2091), will supply membership and benefits at clubs in Britain and abroad.*

*You can enter a gaming house only as a member or a guest of a member. By law, when you join a gaming club you will not be admitted until you have filled in a declaration of your intent to gamble and 48 hours have elapsed from the time you signed this declaration. The number **(48)** after a club's name means this rule applies.*

(M) *means that membership is necessary for entry.*

Annabel's   **4 C3**
44 Berkeley Sq W1. 071-629 2350. Legendary haunt of the rich and famous. Past members have included royals, millionaires and showbiz stars. Long waiting list, but you can get a temporary three-week membership if proposed by an existing member. **(M)**. *Open to 03.00. Closed Sun.*

Charlie Chester Casino (48)   **4 E3**
12 Archer St W1. 071-734 0255. Modern, easy-going nightclub with restaurant and gambling rooms. **(M)**. *Open to 04.00.*

Clermont Club (48)   **4 C3**
44 Berkeley Sq W1. 071-493 5587. An 18thC town house, opulent and comfortable. Select and very expensive to join; a favourite with London's well-heeled businessmen. Excellent restaurant with Arabic cuisine. **(M)**. *Open to 04.00.*

Director's Lodge   **4 D4**
13 Mason's Yard, Duke St SW1. 071-839 6109. Businessmen's club with hostesses. Restaurant with inter-

national cuisine, resident band. **(M)** and entrance fee for guests. *Open to 03.00. Closed Sat & Sun.*

Gaslight of St James's 4 D4

4 Duke of York St SW1. 071-930 1648. Bar, restaurant and hostesses. **(M)** or entrance fee. *Open to 02.00. Closed Sun.*

Morton's 4 C3

28 Berkeley Sq W1. 071-499 0363. Set in a Victorian town house are a late-night disco, bar and restaurant. Attracts wealthy clientele. **(M)**. *Open to 03.00. Closed Sun.*

Stork Club 4 D3

99 Regent St W1. 071-734 1393. Luxury restaurant with dance band and spectacular cabaret. *Open to 03.30. Closed Sun.*

Nightclubs and discotheques

These do not require membership and usually host one-night clubs. As fashions change frequently, it's a good idea to phone the venue or consult Time Out *or* What's On *in advance to check what the correct dress is for that night. Entry to most of the following clubs will be* **£10.00 or under per person.**

Equinox 4 E3

Leicester Sq WC2. 071-437 1446. Full of lights, mirrors, stair-cases, balconies and night owls. Enjoyable and friendly. *Open to 03.30, to 04.00 Fri & Sat. Closed Sun.* A.Ax.V.

Hippodrome 4 E3

Leicester Sq WC2. 071-437 4311. A black cave of brass and chrome illuminated by an amazing lighting system. Six bars, restaurant. *Open to 03.30. Closed Sun.* A.Ax.Dc.V.

Limelight 4 E3

136 Shaftesbury Ave W1. 071-434 0572. Large and lavish club, housed somewhat incongruously in a former Welsh Presbyterian Church. Very popular at weekends. Excellent restaurant. *Open to 03.30. Closed Sun.* A.Ax.Dc.V.

Le Palais

242 Shepherd's Bush Rd W6. 081-748 2812. Very popular mainstream discotheque with glitzy, art-deco furnishing, a restaurant, and a laser show. *Open to 02.00 Wed & Thur, to 03.00 Fri & Sat. Closed Sun, Mon & Tue.* A.Ax.Dc.V.

Stringfellows 4 F3

16 Upper St Martin's Lane WC2. 071-240 5534. Most celebri-ties have been photographed flashing their teeth and jewellery at Stringfellows, but beware – the rich and famous tend to keep themselves to themselves. A la carte restaurant. *Open to 03.30. Closed Sun.* A.Ax.Dc.V.

The Wag 4 E3

35 Wardour St W1. 071-437 5534. Attracts an exuberant, young clientele. Weekend nights are very popular. *Open to 03.30, to 06.00 Fri & Sat. Closed Sun.* No credit cards.

EMERGENCY INFORMATION & SERVICES

ACCIDENT/AMBULANCE
If there's an accident or you need an ambulance for any reason, dial **999** and ask for ambulance.

BABYSITTING AND CHILDCARE
Chelsea Baby Hire
7 Openview SW18. 081-870 5846. Push-chairs, carrycots, car seats etc from one night onwards. Free delivery and collection (central London). Fully qualified nannies available for baby-sitting. Free brochure supplied on request.
Universal Aunts
PO Box 304, Clapham SW4. 071-738 8937. A well-known agency that will provide all kinds of domestic help, including baby-sitters. Office *open 09.30-17.00 Mon-Fri.*

CAR BREAKDOWN
AA (Automobile Association)
Freephone breakdown service 0800 887766. *24 hrs Mon-Sun.* You can call the AA out if your car breaks down, but you will have to join on the spot if you are not already a member. A.V.
National Breakdown
Freephone breakdown service 0800 400600. *24 hrs Mon-Sun.* Non-members will pay more for rescue/recovery than members. A.V.
Olympic Breakdown Service
071-286 8282. *24 hrs Mon-Sun.* An AA and RAC-approved recovery service covering the whole of London. A.Ax.V.
RAC (Royal Automobile Club)
Freephone 0800 828282. *24 hrs Mon-Sun.* You will need to be a member of the RAC, or join when they arrive. A.Ax.V.

CHEMISTS (Late-night)
The local police station keeps a list of chemists and doctors available at all hours.
Bliss Chemist 3 G3
5 Marble Arch W1. 071-723 6116. *Open 09.00-24.00 every*

day of the year. Also at 50-56 Willesden Lane NW6. 071-624 8000. *Open 09.00-24.00 Mon-Sun.*

Boots   **4 E3**
Piccadilly Circus W1. 071-734 6126. *Open 08.30-20.00 Mon-Fri, 09.00-20.00 Sat, 12.00-18.00 Sun.* Also at 75 Queensway W2. 071-229 9266. *Open 09.00-22.00 Mon-Sat.*

Warman Freed
45 Golders Green Rd NW11. 081-455 4351. *Open 08.00-24.00 every day of the year.*

CREDIT CARDS

If you have lost an **Access** *or* **Visa** *card issued by a bank in the UK, contact the emergency number of the issuing bank:*

Barclays
(0604) 230230. *24 hrs.*

Lloyds
(0702) 362988. *24 hrs.*

Midland
081-450 3122. *24 hrs.*

National Westminster
(0532) 778899. *24 hrs.*

Royal Bank of Scotland
(0702) 362988. *24 hrs.*

If you have lost a **Mastercard** *or* **Visa** *card issued abroad, contact the following:*

Mastercard
(0702) 362988. *24 hrs.*

Visa
(0604) 230230. *24 hrs.*

Contact the emergency numbers listed below if you have lost the following cards:

American Express
(0273) 696933. *24 hrs.*

Diners Club
(0252) 516261. *24 hrs.*

Eurocheque card
(0532) 778899. *24 hrs.*

HOSPITALS

Free medical treatment is available under the National Health Service (NHS) to British citizens, students studying courses of six months or more, people who are working in Britain, EC Nationals and visitors from other countries with reciprocal arrangements. **All** other foreign visitors will be required to pay for medical treatment they receive.

24-hour hospital casualty departments
Charing Cross Hospital
Fulham Palace Rd, Hammersmith W6. 081-846 1234.

Guy's Hospital   **5 E4**
St Thomas St SE1. 071-955 5000.
Hammersmith Hospital
Du Cane Rd, Shepherd's Bush W12. 081-743 2030.
Royal Free Hospital
Pond St, Hampstead NW3. 071-794 0500.
Royal London Hospital
Whitechapel Rd, Whitechapel E1. 071-377 7000.
St Bartholomew's Hospital   **5 C1**
West Smithfield EC1. 071-601 8888.
St Thomas's Hospital   **4 G6**
Lambeth Palace Rd SE1. 071-928 9292.
University College Hospital   **1 F5**
Gower St WC1. 071-387 9300.
Westminster Hospital   **7 E2**
Dean Ryle St, Horseferry Rd SW1. 081-746 8000.
Whittington Hospital
Highgate Hill, Archway N19. 071-272 3070.

LATE-NIGHT FOOD
Burger King   **4 E3**
17-21 Leicester Sq WC2. No phone. Member of the well-known chain. Burgers, fries and milkshakes. *Open to 04.00, to 02.00 Sun.*
Harry's   **4 D3**
19 Kingly St W1. 071-434 0309. A nightclubbers' institution. Late-night breakfasts and lively atmosphere. *Open to 06.00.*
Lido   **4 E3**
41 Gerrard St W1. 071-437 4431. Busy and friendly Chinese restaurant. *Open to 05.00.*
Up All Night   **6 C4**
325 Fulham Rd SW10. 071-352 1996. Steaks, burgers and spaghetti served by lively staff. *Open to 06.00.*

LATE POST
Most post offices close at 17.30 Mon-Fri & 12.00 Sat. *However, there is one late opening office in London:*
Post Office   **4 F3**
24-28 William IV St, Trafalgar Sq WC2. 071-930 9580. *Open 08.00-20.00 Mon-Sat.*

LOST PROPERTY
Airports
For property lost in the main airport buildings phone the British Airport Authority's Lost Property Office, Heathrow Airport, Middx. 081-759 4321. Alternatively, contact the individual airport direct (see page 18 for a list of airports).
British Rail (trains)
If you lose something on a train, contact the station where the

train you were on terminates (see page 22 for a list of London British Rail stations). They will be able to inform you whether your belongings have been recovered, and if so, where they have been taken.

London Transport (tubes) 1 B5

Lost Property Office, 200 Baker St W1 (next to Baker St Station). For enquiries about lost property please call in person (or send another person with written authority) or apply by letter. No telephone enquiries. *Open 09.30-14.00 Mon-Fri. Closed Bank hols.*

Taxis

If you leave anything in a taxi, phone the Metropolitan Police Lost Property Office. 071-833 0996. *Open 09.00-16.00 Mon-Fri.*

Passports

Report the loss to the police and to your embassy/high commission.

PUBLIC LAVATORIES

Look out for signs in the street directing you to the nearest public lavatory, or ask someone likely to be familiar with the area; police, traffic wardens, news-vendors and shop-keepers. All public lavatories are divided into separate areas for men and women except the newer cabin-style ones which are found in the street. These are completely self-contained and therefore unisex. They are *open 24 hrs* and you will need exactly the right coins to use them. Nearly all large department stores, museums and national art galleries have lavatories, as do pubs, mainline British Rail stations and several of the central London parks. NB: There are no public lavatories on Underground trains, nor in most Underground stations.

WHEELCLAMPED

If you get wheelclamped, take the label attached to your vehicle, plus the fixed penalty notice, to one of the police car pounds listed below. You will have to pay a (high) fine before the clamp is removed (A.Ax.Dc.V.). It can be some time before someone arrives to remove it, but you must return to and stay with your car. In an emergency telephone 071-252 2222. If you are causing an obstruction your car may be towed away to one of the following pounds. Fines for recovery are very high.

Camden Town Car Pound 1 D2

Oval Rd NW1. *Open 08.00-24.00 Mon-Sat.*

Hyde Park Car Pound 4 B4

NCP Park Lane Car Park, Marble Arch W1. *Open 24 hrs.*

Mount Pleasant Car Pound 2 B5

cnr of Calthorpe St & Farringdon Rd EC1. *Open 08.00-24.00 Mon-Sun.*

Warwick Road Car Pound

245 Warwick Rd, West Kensington W14. *Open 08.00-24.00 Mon-Sat.*